Praise for *Unlock You*

'A truly insightful book. If this doesn't help you achieve your potential, nothing will.'

David Gold, Chair, West Ham United and Gold Group International

'Every individual and business who wants to thrive in the 21st century needs to take care of their and their team's mental health to build resilience and team confidence. This is an important book that guides you to help you, as teams and as people, to deal with uncertain times in an accessible and effective way.'

Dr Jo Twist OBE; CEO, UKIE

'I found *Unlock You* helpful in setting attainable goals for increasing positivity in my life while releasing negativity. It has developed my understanding in areas regarding stress, and enhanced my ability to create a better life for myself using the tools we are naturally designed with.'

Sarah Ali Choudhury, award-winning Indian food expert, Influential Woman of the Year 2018

'Beth Wood and Andy Barker have compiled a fantastic resource with plenty of theory and some inventive ways to practise as you challenge yourself to improve your wellbeing. They don't just help to *Unlock You*, they give you a full set of keys too.'

Ian Martin, cognitive behavioural psychotherapist, The Priory Hospital

'*Unlock You* - the title says everything! So many more of us could live a healthier, more fulfilling and happier life, and this book will unlock your potential. The step-by-step exercises provide the support you'll need to bring positivity and mindfulness into situations we face every day. The research information included explains WHY we need to make adjustments to help change our conditioned thinking and behavioural patterns. It's a book to keep for a lifetime, guiding us through each day as we go forward.'

Mark Curry, actor, presenter, qualified life coach

Unlock You

Pearson

At Pearson, we have a simple mission: to help people make more of their lives through learning.

We combine innovative learning technology with trusted content and educational expertise to provide engaging and effective learning experiences that serve people wherever and whenever they are learning.

From classroom to boardroom, our curriculum materials, digital learning tools and testing programmes help to educate millions of people worldwide – more than any other private enterprise.

Every day our work helps learning flourish and wherever learning flourishes, so do people.

To learn more, please visit us at **www.pearson.com/uk**

Unlock You

BE CALM, CONFIDENT AND HAPPY IN JUST **10** MINUTES A DAY

ANDY BARKER AND BETH WOOD

 Pearson

Harlow, England • London • New York • Boston • San Francisco • Toronto • Sydney • Dubai • Singapore • Hong Kong
Tokyo • Seoul • Taipei • New Delhi • Cape Town • São Paulo • Mexico City • Madrid • Amsterdam • Munich • Paris • Milan

PEARSON EDUCATION LIMITED
KAO Two
KAO Park
Harlow
CM17 9NA
United Kingdom
Tel: +44 (0)1279 623623
Web: www.pearson.com/uk

First edition published 2019 (print and electronic)

ISBN: 978-1-292-25112-7 (print)
        978-1-292-25114-1 (PDF)
        978-1-292-25115-8 (ePub)

British Library Cataloguing-in-Publication Data
A catalogue record for the print edition is available from the British Library

Library of Congress Cataloging-in-Publication Data
A catalog record for the print edition is available from the Library of Congress

10 9 8 7 6 5 4 3 2 1
23 22 21 20 19

Print edition typeset in 10/12pt ITC Giovanni Std by Pearson CSC
Printed by Ashford Colour Press Ltd, Gosport

NOTE THAT ANY PAGE CROSS REFERENCES REFER TO THE PRINT EDITION

Contents

About the authors

Andy Barker is a performance coach and trainer with a diverse background in business and the performing arts. Experience ranging from London West End theatre to senior corporate management fired a fascination with personal development and human behaviour, which led him to train in his specialisation of Cognitive Coaching.

Andy runs two companies: Andy Barker Coaching for his business-based coaching work, and Mind Fitness. He and Mind Fitness co-founder Beth Wood work in organisations of all sizes, in the education and performing arts sectors and in the community. With their teams, they run innovative workshops that train people to increase resilience, reduce anxiety and improve wellbeing.

Beth Wood, together with Andy, developed the Mind Fitness programme which draws upon mindfulness and several cognitive techniques to help people to get out of their own way and achieve their potential. Beth devises the various educational programmes delivered by teams of actor-practitioners to improve the mental health and wellbeing of young people across a range of schools.

With a background in theatre, Beth has written numerous plays and first wrote for Pearson with criticism/drama activities for the Longman's Shakespeare series. In recent years, her focus has been on inclusive theatre, using drama as a developmental tool. As well as Mind Fitness, Beth runs Prospero Theatre, which builds arts programmes and projects around social as well as artistic objectives. She loves every bit of what she does!

Mind Fitness Learning A great day for us at Mind Fitness is when we hear from someone who has attended one of our courses who thanks us and says that they've just got their first job after several months of unemployment. Or a company we work with tells us that after 6 months all their teams are reporting a boost in performance and increased levels of engagement.

Our aim, with this book as with all our training work, is to help people to feel and work better.

Our work takes the Mind Fitness teams to a wide variety of organisations from tiny charities to huge corporates. Sometimes we are starting from scratch, helping an organisation to develop strategy; other times we are a small part of an existing and robust programme to boost performance and support wellbeing. Both are equally exciting.

We also work extensively in the performance sector, with drama schools, theatre companies and individuals. In the education sector we have teams in primary, secondary and special schools in an extensive programme funded by Children in Need. And we tour Unlock You Live, open events for individuals to attend.

We work wherever we can make a difference.

For details of our work with **Organisations**, in **Performance** or **Education** please visit our website www.mindfitness.training

Acknowledgements

Andy Barker: Huge thanks to Zena Everett and Ian Martin for the inspiration, David Newth for the guidance, and immense gratitude to my family for their constant, unwavering support. Thank you too Beth, for being a brilliant editor, collaborator and business partner.

Beth Wood: Massive thanks to Jess Clements for the beginnings of this journey, to Lyn Robinson, Rebecca Riley, Tina Slaughter for practical support and to Jess Schofield-Wood for all kinds of support. Thank you to Andy for the adventure that is Mind Fitness.

Both Andy and Beth would like to thank our editor Eloise Cook for her encouragement, patience and insight.

Publisher's acknowledgements

Images:

30 Shutterstock: Lightspring/Shutterstock **36 Shutterstock:** Andrea Danti/Shutterstock **94 Springer Publishing Company:** Lazarus AA (1977) 'Towards an egoless state of being', found in A Ellis and R Grieger, eds., Handbook of Rational-Emotive Therapy, Springer Pub Co (1 Dec. 1977). **112 Shutterstock:** metamorworks/Shutterstock

Text:

40 Elizabeth Carter: Epictetus. **40 Meric Casaubon:** Marcus Aurelius. 40 William Shakespeare: Hamlet , Full text: http://shakespeare.mit.edu/hamlet/full.html **89 Abraham Lincoln:** Abraham Lincoln **106 Apud Ludovicum Elzevirium:** Descartes, R (1644). Renati Des-Cartes Principia philosophiæ [With illustrations.]. Apud Ludovicum Elzevirium: Amstelodami. **122 Houghton Mifflin Harcourt:** Napoleon Bonaparte's writings compiled by R.M. Johnston (in The Corsican: A Diary of Napoleon's Life in His Own Words, 1910).. **122 Penguin Group:** Psycho-Cybernetics Deluxe Edition: The Original Text of the Classic Guide to a New Life, Maxwell Maltz, Penguin, 2016. **136 The British Library Board:** Palmer S, Cooper C, Thomas K (2003). Creating a balance: Managing stress. London: British Library **156 Franklin D Roosevelt:** Franklin D Roosevelt. **156 Pearson education Ltd:** Thomas Jonathan Jackson (1824–1863) zitiert in "Memoirs of Stonewall Jackson by His Widow, Mary Anna Jackson", Prentice Press/Courier Journal, 1895 156 Abraham Lincoln: Abraham Lincoln

Preface

We have spent several years developing the Mind Fitness programme which we and our teams use to work with businesses, performers, individuals and community groups. There are plenty of exercises through the book, and other exercises and resources on our website www.mindfitness.training. Our aim is to share the programme with as many people as we can and so we are delighted to be able to welcome you to *Unlock You.*

Andy Barker and Beth Wood

Introduction

You are beginning a fantastic journey. Our aim is that when you finish this programme, you will be more calm, confident and happy. You will be achieving many more of the things you want to achieve because you will have stopped getting in your own way. Your time won't be eaten up by negative thoughts and worries that plunge you into a downward spiral. You will be more understanding of those around you and more appreciative of the things you have in your life. Perhaps, most importantly, you will have changed, changed in a way that releases enormous amounts of potential. You'll be able to look at yourself and say 'Wow! Yes of course. This is who I am.'

This is a practical book that will give you practical benefits, and here's a list of what's possible:

▶ You'll be able to recognise a negative or unhelpful belief and be able to replace it with a more positive one.

▶ You'll learn how to remain focussed and not let the automatic negative thoughts take over. (We call these the ANTs.)

▶ You'll understand what kinds of stress are good (the buzz, being in a state of flow) and what kinds are bad. You'll know how to identify the line and re-cross if necessary.

▶ You'll be able to recognise the physical symptoms of 'fight or flight mode' and know simple techniques to place you back in a state in which the higher thinking brain can properly function.

▶ You'll understand what emotional and cognitive states are conducive to new learning (the zone of proximal development) and know techniques to enter and 'stretch' this zone.

▶ You'll be able to set goals that are attainable and in line with your beliefs.

▶ You'll understand which emotions are negative and unhealthy. You'll learn how to sit with them, accept them and work to change them.

▶ You'll learn how integral positivity and creativity are to the state of wellbeing and how focussed attention can be used to release creative potential.

In short, you'll learn to get out of your own way and realise that life can be a whole lot better than you thought!

How does it work?

So, how does this programme work? And how much work will be involved in order to reap such amazing benefits?

We call this programme Mind Fitness. Think of it as a personal trainer for your mind. In the same way as you would work on physical fitness, the programme will give you easy to use exercises to declutter and refocus your brain. And, once you're fit you need to stay fit, so the book will show you how to do this. We all have enormous amounts of potential that we don't use, that become buried under the debris of our stressful lives. This really is about unlocking the best possible you.

Mind Fitness draws on cognitive behavioural therapy (CBT) and mindfulness to deliver an effective programme that is easy to build into your daily life. The way it works is basically this: CBT, as many of you will know, is about challenging and changing our unhelpful beliefs. But we've sometimes had these beliefs for a very long time and so our instinct is to defend them. What mindfulness does, because it teaches us to be reflective rather than reflexive by bringing a calm attention to the present moment, is buy us the time and the space in which to make those big changes. Very often, our first impulsive response to an event is not the one that will bring us the most benefit. But you will find that, as your new way of thinking becomes habit, this will change.

The Mind Fitness programme draws extensively upon the imagination. There is strong research to show that our imagination is closely linked to our higher thinking brain and our ability to focus and solve problems.[1] It doesn't mean that you have to become Picasso for this to work, though there are probably worse ways of using your free time and there's stacks of good stuff in the creative therapies. But no, we'll just be asking you to think about things, to put images in your mind, and to imagine events and situations.

How should I work through this programme?

Is it then possible to pick and choose chapters and hone in on those that are most relevant? Well, yes you can do that and you would still get something out of it, but not nearly as much as if you follow it through chapter by chapter. You will, through the book, learn to be your own coach, even, to some extent, your own therapist. You will build up a range of tools and techniques that you can employ when times get tough, but that are equally useful in giving you that little extra push to be more confident, more willing to jump, to dance, to laugh and to love.

We hope that by the time you have read this book you will be well on the way to being Mind Fit. To consolidate these changes, the final chapter includes a six-week follow-up programme. It brings together some of the key tools from the book, with plenty of choice so that you can select the exercises that work best for you. These are structured into a few minutes of practice in the morning and a few minutes at night, with a few guided check-ins during the day to keep you aware of your new thinking. By the time you have finished the book and the six-week follow-up, the techniques will be fully embedded and you will hardly be aware of them. They will underpin a new daily routine, a new way of seeing yourself and the world. There will be times, of course, where that new world is rocked by unforeseen circumstances and events, but you will be able to cope. You'll know what to do to get yourself back on your feet.

What else will it involve? In each chapter, there will be slices of learning followed by exercises where you can test out what you have learned and see how it makes you feel.

We don't want you to focus on the exercises when using this book; it's equally important to read the theory, because we want to help you to change your unhelpful thinking, and that means understanding why your thinking should change. You don't have to take a degree in neuroscience, just to have a basic idea of the how and the why. It's when you get the 'aha' feeling, the moment of 'getting it', that the defences go down and the new ideas and habits begin.

Scientists used to believe that the brain was hardwired by the time you became an adult and that, from then on, only a minimal amount of change was possible.[2] We now know that is not true. We will explain how and why in the section on neuroplasticity. So what we are doing together through this book is rewiring your brain. That is not nearly as scary as it sounds. We will be discovering all the wonderful things that make you *you*, and letting go of the negative thoughts, emotions and ideas that have somehow clung to you over the years. So often we aren't even aware that it is these that are making us feel anxious or sad and impeding our progress.

So, in each chapter we will be telling you just enough about the what and the why and then you will try it out! People that we work with when we are training tell us that they come to love the science bits. Almost everyone has had moments of being fascinated by the human brain. Up to 60,000 thoughts a day.[3] 100,000 chemical reactions every second![4] Who wouldn't be fascinated? And we are living at an incredible time where neuroscience is pushing forward at a rate something like the IT revolution of the last two decades. Everything we do in this programme is evidenced by science. Much of that would not have been possible even 10 years ago.

We're going to learn about CBT later in the book. We'll look at mindfulness now.

What is mindfulness?

Mindfulness has its roots in Buddhist meditation, although the practice of meditating has been widely used in many cultures throughout the ages. The modern mindfulness movement has a spiritual side and a science-based side (although it can be said that, with the expansion of neuroscience, these two arms seem to be pulling towards each other.) This book is rooted in the science-based side of mindfulness, although we have the utmost respect for the spiritual arm. People will be coming to this book from all sorts of cultures and systems of belief. These spiritual beliefs are not necessary, but neither will they inhibit your progress.

A simple definition is that mindfulness brings our attention to the present moment in order to experience life more clearly and more fully. The benefits of mindfulness practice have been evidenced in the many research studies from the top international universities.[5] They include a reduction in stress and an increased level of emotional control; a general and often profound sense of wellbeing and an increase in positivity and motivation.

It's worth thinking about what we mean by 'more clearly and more fully'. How do we experience life more clearly and more fully? First task for you, then. Tomorrow try looking out, all day, for the colour blue. Not only will you see more blue than you dreamed existed, but the colour itself will get more and more blue through the day. One of the real and valuable benefits from this programme is that your sensory input will be sharper than it has ever been, because the brain works much more effectively when it is focussed on only one task. I hear bird song and I notice butterflies and I taste my food. Andy says that the simple task of taking his dogs for a walk has been completely transformed. It's extraordinary how much richer a world you will be living in, and how much this alone helps you on the journey towards cup half full.

Just a little bit of science before we embark on the next exercise. Two extraordinary facts about the brain that are at the core of this programme.

The first we have mentioned before – it is generally accepted that we have about 20–60,000 thoughts a day. Isn't that incredible? Equally incredible is the fact that only a very small percentage of these are focussed on the task at hand, the activity we are doing at that moment. We'll talk later about where the rest of those thoughts are going and learn some brilliant techniques to call more of our brain power to task.

The second is that a part of our brain, the amygdala, instigates our fight or flight stress response when we perceive threat or danger. Once we are in fight or flight, the amygdala stops passing information to our higher thinking brain, so, at times of stress, say an exam or interview, when we most need to be thinking clearly, decision making, problem solving, we literally can't.

Through the book, you'll learn to get yourself out of the frozen state and regain the faculties you need to use. Once you are very practised, you may even beat the amygdala to it, activating the process of relaxation before the fight or flight kicks in. We always say to people new to the programme, if there was just one reason why everyone should do this, it would be that. Most of the occasions in our personal and professional lives when we really need to think clearly are going to involve some level of stress or perceived stress. We'll look at how the brain perceives this stress in Chapter 10. The programme has helped people with exam nerves, stage fright and presentation phobias as well as dealing with any number of other issues concerned with anxiety. Staying in a state of fight or flight leads to constant, chronic stress, the consequences of which can be life threatening.

So mindfulness-based exercises centre around the practice of being in the moment. Much mindfulness work centres around the breath. The senses are also excellent. Always remember that our senses work only in the present. If you ever need to ground yourself just for a moment, simply concentrating on any one of the senses, something you can see or hear, the sensation of something you are touching or holding, or on the breath, almost always will do the trick.

When we are training, we find that some people respond best to the exercises using hearing, others to more visual or sensory exercises. As you learn the exercises, be aware of what feels best for you.

This first exercise is called Circles of Attention. It brings your attention into the present moment by focusing on the sounds that you can hear within different circles of attention.

Exercise 1: Circles of Attention

Begin by getting yourself as comfortable as possible, either sitting or lying down. If you are sitting, make sure that you have legs uncrossed and hands either on your lap or on your knees. Take a minute to just be aware of the parts of your body that have contact with the chair or with the floor. This will bring your attention into the present moment. Take two breaths, slightly deeper than you would normally take, breathing in through the nose and out through the mouth.

Now close your eyes and listen as carefully as you can to any sounds that you can hear coming from inside your body. Every 30 seconds or so you are going to move your attention to the next circle. The sequence goes:

- ▶ Listening to sounds from inside your body
- ▶ Listening to sounds from inside the room
- ▶ Listening to sounds from outside the room
- ▶ Listening to sounds from inside the room
- ▶ Listening to sounds from inside your body

Almost certainly you will find that other thoughts come into your mind. Don't worry about this at all. At this stage, just gently let them move away and bring your attention back to the sounds you are listening to. We will talk about this 'noise', or automatic thoughts, in detail as you move through the programme.

The whole exercise should take between three and five minutes.

After the exercise, have a moment to think about how you felt during and after it. Many people have the sense of a weight being lifted or the sense of being in touch right from the first time of doing a mindfulness-based exercise. If this hasn't happened for you, don't worry. Certainly the benefits grow as you deepen your practice and learn to use the exercises in conjunction with the cognitive behavioural therapy (CBT) based techniques.

The kind of focus you employed in the exercise is listening with effort. We all do it when it's something we are really interested in. When I am training I use this example – 'If I said, I am going to tell you three things and, if you can remember them at the end of the session, I'll give you a tenner – you would all listen in such a way that they were imprinted in your mind'. Everyone always knows just what I mean! That is 'listening' with effort, sometimes called attending. If we can do it when we apply ourselves to it – we can do it all the time. Even better, we can do it when we really need to. So often it is when, say, we go to the doctors that we really need to hear what we are being told, but, because we are stressed, our fight or flight kicks in and we come out with very little idea of what was said.

We are going to do a short practical recap of this foreword by revisiting five simple statements. After each statement just write the first word or phrase that comes in to your mind. It doesn't matter if it is a factual response, an emotional response, a hope or wish, a note of how it relates to you, or anything else. It is partly to see what you remember, what stuck in your mind, but it will also get you used to having an active creative response. That is very much the ethos of this programme. The more active and creative you are, the faster and deeper it will work.

Exercise 2: Chapter Recap

1 Your time will not be eaten up by negative thoughts and worries that plunge you into a downward spiral.

   Word or phrase_____

2 Mindfulness teaches us to be reflective rather than reflexive.

   Word or phrase_____

3 Mindfulness brings your attention to the present in order to experience life more clearly and more fully.

   Word or phrase_____

4 Our amygdala instigates our fight or flight response which stops any information getting to our higher thinking brain.

   Word or phrase_____

5 Thanks to neuroscience, we know now that our beliefs, habits and attitudes can be changed right up to the end of our lives.

   Word or phrase_____

Mind Fitness, then, is a mixture of mindfulness and cognitive skills woven together by practical exercises, many of which employ the use of the imagination. It is not time-consuming, can be built into your daily life and anyone can do it.

As you move into Chapter 1, we'd like you to invest in a notebook in which you can jot down anything that seems important to you as you go along. It's good to have notes that you can come back to as you learn more about the process. The foundations are laid and the journey begins. Have fun.

1

Focus on what you want

How to make what's important to you move to the centre of your life and how to use it to boost your resilience

There are some fantastic books on resilience and a number of trainers delivering pretty good courses. We have been to a fair few of them and it is likely that some of you have too. So why is this different?

Well, as you know from the introductory chapter, CBT is all about beliefs. The things that we believe in are vitally important to our sense of self and our understanding of who we are. All too many of us, however, go about our daily lives virtually ignoring the beliefs that shape and define us. So many people say that x (music, philanthropy, justice, any number of things) is massively important to them, and yet x plays little or no part in their life. It is a clear case of self-neglect! Not only that, but, if you are trying to pursue goals that are at odds with these beliefs, they are likely to have become invisible obstacles tugging you back when you are trying so hard to move forwards. In short, they will be making it inevitable that you are getting in your own way.

They will also be undermining your resilience. By the end of this book, you will have become aware of many of your unhelpful beliefs and, of course, a few helpful ones too, which is a bonus. You will have refocussed the unhelpful beliefs to be more helpful or ditched them if you do not need them. As a result, your level of resilience will have increased manifold. Sounds like dark and dangerous work? Well, the great news is that it's not.

What do we mean by resilience?

So, let's make sure we are all on the same page. What do you we mean by resilience? In our society it's a quality that is pretty much universally admired, but often we have quite different versions of it in our wonderfully uniquely constructed minds.

Exercise 1.1: Resilience Award

We said that Mind Fitness is a programme that makes full use of the imagination. We would like you to take a piece of paper or your mindfulness notebook, if you've had time to buy one, and close your eyes. We want you to decide who you would nominate for a Resilience Award. It can be a famous person, someone known for their courage or endurance, but also it can be your friend or your mum. Anyone at all. Now have two minutes to think about what it is about them, or the actions they have taken, that gives them extreme resilience, as you have defined it in your mind. Jot down a few notes.

Now have a look at your notes and see what qualities you have identified as most important. Often people choose individuals who have gone through extreme adversity and come through it with increased strength. Some of the words and phrases commonly used are:

- Endurance
- Bravery
- Resolve
- Determination
- Spirit
- Bouncing back

Let's take a moment to consider why we need this resilience. What does it give us that enables us to survive – no, better, to thrive? It is generally accepted that we need resilience to:

- Control pressure
- Better manage anxiety
- Reduce the risk of suffering chronic long-term stress
- Strengthen emotional intelligence
- Have a greater sense of wellbeing
- Manage challenging relationships
- Improve performance and productivity
- Be able to adapt to change
- Be able to confront adversity

Somewhere in there is probably the reason why you bought this book, so resilience is obviously very important. Resilience to what? When do we need to use this resilience? Take a minute after each of the following to consider how you might have shown resilience or lack of it in each of these scenarios:

- ▶ A big event (for example a wedding, divorce, house move, bereavement)
- ▶ A minor event or series of events that seemed challenging (for example late trains, lost keys, a financial loss)
- ▶ Ongoing adversity (for example long-term illness of yourself or a loved one)
- ▶ Day-to-day annoyances that tend to trip us up

Try to be specific and identify an actual scenario – something with which you have had to contend.

Considering your answers, take a moment to think about how resilient you would say that you are now, so that you have something to compare it with at the end of this book. Score yourself out of 10. Of course, most of us are more resilient in some situations than others. We all know someone who is ferociously able to cope in the working environment but falls to pieces in a home situation. And the reverse. This will be linked to where they place the meaning in their life, which we will come back to later.

What does a resilient response to a situation look like?

Next we're going to do a quick exercise to think about how we behave when we are feeling resilient (or not) – how resilience expresses itself in everyday life.

Is resilience really something you can develop? Yes absolutely.

Exercise 1.2: Respond with Resilience

Write out three simple situations from your work or home life that would require resilience.

Then give a non-resilient and a resilient response to each of the situations.

For example:

Your boss was supposed to give a talk this afternoon but she has gone home ill and, on her way out, told you that you would have to cover.

Non-resilient response – There is no way I can do it! I don't know enough! I will make a fool of myself!

Resilient response – Well it could be a great opportunity if I do it well. I know most of it and I have a couple of hours to prepare.

1 Situation:

   Non-resilient response:

   Resilient response:

2 Situation:

   Non-resilient response:

   Resilient response:

3 Situation:

   Non-resilient response:

   Resilient response:

Is resilience really something you can develop? Yes absolutely.

What underpins and powers our resilience?

People used to think that resilience is something we are born with, that we either have or don't. But since we have known about neuroplasticity (which we will be looking at in Chapter 3), we know that we can change the way our brain works and this includes developing and strengthening resilience.

The way we respond to an event or situation depends on our beliefs and attitudes and the meaning that we attach to them. This is why a group of people will respond to the same event in any number of different ways. This is a key concept that we will revisit several times in the book. Think of a situation such as a mass redundancy. One person might see the redundancy as an absolute disaster. To another it might be a bump in the road, even an opportunity.

It is interesting when we look at figures who have shown this resilience, this invincibility, that, in very many cases, there is a deep meaning at their core.

They have something so strong that they believe in, that has literally powered them through the darkest of situations. I (BW) had the honour of meeting Terry Waite, who was held as a hostage for four years in the Lebanon. This meaning that had 'helped him through' was almost palpable. When I met him in 2012, he had just returned to Beirut to be reconciled with his captors.

Perhaps the most extreme case of this is that of Viktor Frankl who wrote the seminal book on resilience *Man's Search for Meaning* after being a prisoner in Auschwitz.[1] If resilience is something you want to focus on, you can do no better than read this. Actually everyone should read this; we all need good regular doses of inspiration.

Thankfully, most of us do not undergo traumas on such a monumental scale, but the same principle applies. If you can identify what is most important to you and bring it to the centre of your life, then everything else begins to fall into place around it. And when we say what is most important to you, we mean important to you now – not when you last thought about it which may be way back in the mists of time. We trained a lovely and extremely clever woman whose face fell as she reeled off her beliefs. It started with passion and ended in absolute confusion as she realised she had stated this list of beliefs to a lecturer at university whom she wanted badly to impress. Not only had she not revisited it in 22 years, though she had 'repeated' it often, but it had not even been soundly true at the time. She had told him what she thought he wanted to hear.

To some extent, this is true of most of us. We are loathe to change our fundamental beliefs. After all, if we start to mess around with them, where would we be? In fact, who would we be? Surely our identity would start to peel like an onion?

It will not! It will grow exponentially – because the beliefs you will have at the end of the process will be real. They will suit you now – suit you and your purpose, suit your goals, and then you will be free to go on to really achieve.

Most, if not all of us, are creatures of habit, resistant to change. Foods we hated in our childhood we will continue to avoid without ever seeing if our tastes have changed. Our instinct to 'stick with' is even stronger with beliefs.

What is a belief?

We've been talking since the beginning of the book about beliefs. Before we go on, let's think about what we mean by a belief.

A belief can be a broad belief, for example relating to politics, religion, race, gender, sexuality, life choices, human rights or the law. Or it can be a specific belief relating to people, situations or aspects of your life.

We are going to ask you now to take the first step of identifying a fundamental belief, something that has a profound effect on the life you lead and the choices you make.

We're leading in with a mindfulness exercise to place you into the best possible learning state.

Exercise 1.3: Image Breathing

This exercise is called Image Breathing. We will do it a few times through the programme, each time with a slightly deeper application.

As with many of our exercises, Image Breathing employs the imagination. It attaches the breath to calming or reassuring personalised mental images.

Again, begin by getting yourself as comfortable as possible, either sitting or lying down. If you are sitting, make sure that you have legs uncrossed and hands either on your lap or on your knees. Take a moment to just be aware of the parts of your body that have contact with the chair or with the floor. Take two breaths, slightly deeper than you would normally take, breathing in through the nose and out through the mouth.

As this is the first time that you have done the exercise, rather than choose your own image, we'd like you to think of a beautiful beach on a sunny day. You are standing in the sea looking in towards the land. On each breath in, imagine the water gathering and, on each breath out, imagine that your breath is pushing the wave up onto the beach.

We're going to take four breaths. Keep focussed on the image of the beach. Really use your imagination – think of the details of what it is that you are seeing. What colour is the sand? What is the weather like? Can you see anything beyond the beach? How cold is the water? If any other thoughts come into your mind while you are doing the exercise, let them gently drift away and take your attention back to the image.

▶ Breathe in. And out.

▶ Breathe in. And out.

▶ Breathe in. And out.

▶ Breathe in. And out.

Exercise 1.4: Long-held Beliefs

Take a moment to jot down a few of the most important and long-held beliefs you hold. Then, next to the belief, write down when you started believing it and when was the last time, if ever, that you revisited the belief.

Exercise 1.5: Identifying a Key Belief

With your eyes still closed, identify a belief that you hold, something that you hold dear or something that, thinking about it now, you realise has shaped and defined you and your life in some way. Write it down.

That is your first step in a very exciting and liberating journey. As you dig down, you will find that at the centre of resilience is the important trio of belief, attitude and meaning.

The heart of resilience

For a few days, try to be aware of the beliefs that you hold, the attitudes you have to the important things in your life and the things that give your life meaning.

As with mindfulness, it's really about noticing, learning to spot and identify your beliefs. There are probably beliefs that you hold that, deep down, you know are there. Others will pop up and absolutely surprise you. We humans have beliefs about some pretty crazy things. When we're training, Andy talks about one of his, which is the belief that, after you knock or ring the bell to go into someone's house, you *must* step back from the step before they get to the door! And we've learned that a belief that seems ridiculous to one person will seem perfectly sensible to someone else.

Recognising a belief

It may be useful to think about how a belief is expressed:

▶ Thought
▶ Emotion
▶ Behaviour

We find it's easiest to unpick if you think, for a moment, about anyone on TV or in public life who drives you mad – we all have one. So, for this person, it may break down as:

Thought – I think x is an idiot (feel free to substitute stronger language!).

Emotion – x makes me feel angry every time I see them.

Behaviour – I turn off the television every time x comes on.

Take the important belief that you wrote down and see if you can think about how it is expressed – thought, emotion, behaviour. Write these out:

▶ Thought
▶ Emotion
▶ Behaviour

Meaning

Now focus for a moment on meaning.

We said that, over the course, you would gradually identify the beliefs that are most helpful and most important to you and bring them to the centre of your life. If you can marry your deepest beliefs, your meaning, your values, with your goals, then your objectives become so much easier to achieve.

This is where you identify your meaning. Again, we will come back to this several times in the book.

Exercise 1.6: Meaning

As a starting point, go back to all the different beliefs you have thought about during this chapter, write them down, if you haven't already, and put a tick beside them if, generally, the belief makes you happy, or a cross if, generally, it doesn't.

Now put another tick by those that you think are closely tied to what gives meaning to your life.

And, finally, make a statement about that meaning. For some people, this may be conceptual – 'doing good', 'making a difference', for others it may be much more specific – 'protecting my family'.

In each chapter, we'll put in a couple of frequently asked questions. Others can be found on our website.

Questions and Answers

▶ **Increasing resilience is all very well, but shouldn't people just 'man up'? That's the simplest way, right?**

We would argue that this approach creates more issues than it solves. The Mind Fitness approach is around flexibility, being able to change. Invest the time in what is causing an issue and it will be solved rather than papered over.

▶ **I can't honestly say that I can pinpoint 'meaning' as such in my life. I go to work and come home. Watch a bit of telly. I just get on with it. Is this unusual? Why don't I have something that others seem to?**

Meaning in life doesn't have to be about big, profound things. It can be about the importance you place in doing your job well. It can be time spent with mates down the pub. A shared game of footy. A night out with the girls. A family meal. The things that we value. Simple pleasures or an important cause that's central to who you are. It's all based on meaning.

Exercise 1.7: Chapter Recap

What have we learned?

A short practical exercise to reinforce what we have covered. You can close your eyes if it helps.

1 Bring to mind the faces of three resilient people

2 Locate a situation in which you demonstrated resilience

3 Three key factors in determining resilience are belief, meaning and ...

4 Remind yourself of how you felt after the Image Breathing exercise

5 Give an example of a broad belief you have now or have had in the past

6 Give an example of a specific belief you have now or have had in the past

7 Why do you think you are likely to have more resilience if you are in touch with what gives your life meaning?

8 Think about a belief that you hold that has brought you great joy

Conclusion

You have begun the process of identifying your beliefs and the things that are most important to you. We'll go on to learn how you can make sure that your central beliefs are helpful, to find ways to change or refocus the ones that are not, and to tie these beliefs to your goals and ambitions. Gradually, you will learn to side-step when you are in danger of getting in your own way, until finally you will see the world through the eyes of the best possible you.

Get to know your brain

How that wonderful brain of yours works and how to make it your friend

In this chapter, we'll look at the way your remarkable brain functions, learn to identify some of the triggers that lead you to self-sabotage and begin the process of harnessing your enormous potential. We like to think of it as making friends with your brain. And, in order to make friends with someone, or in this case something, we need to get to know it a little better.

There is still a lot that we don't know about the brain and how it functions but we are lucky to be living now. The amount that we do know has exploded over the last 10 years. But, before we look at the amazing things that a brain can do, we need, perhaps, to think about the important concept lurking beneath the idea of making friends. You are not your brain.

For any of you who hold religious or spiritual beliefs, that statement will be a given. For others who live in a more secular universe, it can be quite disorienting. A question we have been asked often when we're leading training sessions is 'But surely I am my mind?' or even the inevitable follow-on 'If I am not my mind, who am I?'

Either way – no, you are not your mind. One of the most important maxims to remember is that you don't have to believe what you think. Take a moment to say that to yourself slowly – you don't have to believe what you think. Just because your mind misbehaves occasionally and tells you that all the people in your office became a little quieter than usual as you walked in – and that must, of course, be because they were talking about you – you don't have to believe it, let alone act upon it. During the programme, we'll teach you how to notice and explore your thoughts in a more detached way and reframe the ones that have led, in the past, to needless upset, self-sabotage and lost opportunities.

All we can say is that, if answering this question is important to you, then you will be in the best possible place to begin your quest by the end of this book. Or perhaps you will find that, as your positivity and confidence grow, you will gain a sense of self that provides you with all you need.

How your amazing brain works

Your brain is a truly amazing organ, a kind of biological computer, with a complex and wonderful communications system. The briefest of descriptions about how it works.

Your brain, spinal cord and peripheral nerves make up a complex, integrated information-processing and control system known as your central nervous system. Together, they regulate all the conscious and unconscious facets of your life, from your thoughts, ideas and physical movements to your dreams.

The brain consists of about 100 billion neurons, which need to communicate with each other over minute distances. Each message sent uses electrical activity and is called a neural impulse. The gap between the neurons is called a synapse, so the message (or impulse) crosses these gaps. There are from 1,000 to 10,000 synapses for each neuron.[1]

The capacity, to which you have access, is colossal. To achieve everything outlined in this book is easily possible for you with the help of this monumental assistant. To give you an idea of the magnitude, scientists postulate that the processing speed of the human brain is a billion billion (called 1 exaFLOP) calculations per second. And, just as incredible, unlike modern supercomputers which have to use enough servers to fill a small city and use enough energy to power 10,000 homes, the human brain consumes less energy than a dim light bulb and fits beautifully into the human head.

Our brain developed, through evolution, to help us to survive. If we couldn't be the most frightening or the fastest, we'd be the smartest. And when basic survival was paramount it all worked well. The brain was the servant and it produced top-class information that led to lots of eating and procreating and the avoidance of more wild beasts than we can imagine. For many of us, however, because of a combination of information overload and the huge number of things about which we can be anxious or worried, that relationship has been turned upside down. The brain has become the master and it sends us off on roads that lead to the large-scale wasting of time, to untenable levels of stress and anxiety and, for some people, real trauma and pain. It's a vicious circle; more worries means less control, less control means more worries. It's time to hold out the olive branch.

The first stage of making friends with your wonderful brain is to begin the journey towards awareness. What is your brain doing this very minute? How does it spend its time? Has your mind wandered to other things, even while you've been reading this chapter? There is *no* shame in this; this is where the punishment stops!

Exercise 2.1: Image Breathing

To begin the process of awareness, we're going to do the Image Breathing exercise from Chapter 1 (page 7), but on a slightly deeper level. This time, you are going to think of your own image, something that means something to you.

We have a golfer friend, for example, who imagines on the in-breath the golf club swinging back. The out-breath is the club hitting the ball and the ball being propelled, by the breath, into the distance.

Choose an image now that you feel would work for you. And, if it doesn't work this time, change it. If you can't think of an image, just focus again on the wave on the beach, but this time adding more detail to the picture. Take the four breaths.

Consider how easy or difficult you found the exercise. Stay comfortable and relaxed; we're going to do it one more time, but this time, if your mind wanders, notice the thought or thoughts for a moment before you let them slip away. After the exercise, open your eyes, keeping the feelings of relaxation and focus.

Noise

Gradually, as you move through the programme, you'll learn to notice thoughts, without letting them damage or control you. If something comes into your mind fairly often, then it is likely that it is a thought that is worthy of some rational consideration. But you don't have to do its bidding. And you don't have to get caught up in the negative spiral of one thought leading to another, bringing up the emotion of a past experience, and so on. This is what we are going to look at next. Mind Fitness is never about suppressing the negative. Apart from anything else, keeping the lid on negative thoughts and emotions is a truly exhausting process. You can spend all your energy ignoring a thought that's hammering at your mind, trying to get in. It feels huge, so loud that you are sure that it will drown you, but, surprisingly, once you recognise that it's there, it almost always loses its volume and vehemence.

There is a great mini-exercise that you can do to get yourself used to noticing without following the trail. Stand somewhere you can see cars passing. Let yourself notice them without following them. I love to do this with boats on the banks of the Thames. We call these automatic negative thoughts ANTs. You won't stamp them out; having them is part of being human, but you can learn techniques so that the ANTs don't overrun your wonderful mind.

You may find that a persistent obtrusive thought is linked to an unhelpful belief that needs to be picked out from the line-up when we get to Chapter 4. Many people find that it is when meditating or doing a mind-fulness-based exercise that these unhelpful beliefs make themselves known.

So where do these thoughts come from? We said that the average person has up to 60,000 thoughts a day and that only a very small percentage, perhaps 5 per cent, are 'spent' on the activity or task in hand. The rest of the thoughts that come cluttering are referred to as Noise.

Past-Future Noise

There are two main kinds of Noise. The first is Past-Future Noise and the second is Negative Self-Talk. We're going to look first at Past-Future Noise. We said that mindfulness is bringing our attention to the present moment in order to experience life more clearly and more fully. Contrasted with that is the almost universal tendency of dwelling on the past and thinking forward to the future or potential futures. Clinical psychologists state that worrying about the past leads to depression and worrying about the future to acute anxiety.[2] In prehistoric times, when the dangers, although incredibly real, could be counted on one hand, they were dealt with as and when they presented themselves. Now we have so many worries that our brain labels as 'dangers' that we are constantly on alert, constantly scanning our past experiences for errors and mistakes, constantly anxious about what is to come.

Worrying about the past

Across all cultures, a common part of the human experience is to replay situations or events in our minds, often reworking them slightly so that we gradually take on a stronger role, defend our position, win an argument or let people know what we really think. While a certain amount of calm, balanced reflection is positive, allowing us to learn from our experiences and to realise when we have moved off course and begin to course-correct, this kind of 'if only' replaying is almost always negative. It results in the negative emotions we felt being brought from the past into the present and being painfully re-experienced. It can lead to the sensation of being trapped in the situation. This worrying about the past is called ruminating.

It is often said that successful people consider their failures fully but as quickly as possible; once they have learned any lessons, they move speedily on to the course-correct. Instead of dwelling on past failure, they will dwell on past success.

For others it is all too easy to let past problems take a weighty control of our lives. It leads to 'why?' and 'why me?' thinking. We all know people whose identity is so closely rolled up in their problems that the problems have become who they are.

Certainly, there is only one way to make sure that our future is better than our past. That is to accept who and where we are and, in this moment, this present, make changes.

Worrying about the future

The other part of Past-Future Noise is the equally vast amount of time we spend worrying about the future, in fact, worrying about possible futures. It is, essentially, 'what if?' thinking. Too many of us look back at the end of our lives and realise that we spent a great deal of time worrying about things that never happened.

So why do we spend so much time on this worry? It is psychological fear, fear of something that might happen, not of something that is happening to you now. Often, your brain recalls similar situations, or the most similar it can find, that have caused you anxiety and blends them up into a stew of potential trauma that would blight the resilience of the toughest individual. And that is perfectly natural. When it comes to protecting you, the brain only has the past to go on. In a situation of extreme and complex danger, say a battlefield, this would be incredibly useful. In day-to-day life, it's best to give it a smile of recognition and let it go.

It is easy to forget the simple fact that we make our future by what we do in the present. If we are filling our present with future worries and fear, this will be in the ground plan moving forwards, and so it becomes a self-fulfilling prophecy. Our fears and worries are intrinsically linked to the negative beliefs we have about ourselves and, as we learn to draw these out into the open and to challenge and change them, the future-based Noise will shrink and lose its power.

That isn't to say that we can or should ignore all thoughts about the future. A certain amount of planning is necessary and, in fact, makes life a whole lot less stressful. We have found, for example, in our work with businesses, that some managers and directors are supremely good at planning in their organisation, but don't use these skills at all when it comes to their personal life and goals.

With both Past and Future Noise, to get lost in these thoughts is the mind becoming master. The worry kicks in and one negative thought moves on to another; this introduces an even worse imagined possibility or another threat or anxiety, and so on. As we mentioned before, we call these automatic negative thoughts ANTs. Don't let the ANTs steal your brain!

The first stage is recognising that this spiral is starting and realising that just because the possibility of x happening has entered your mind and latched on strongly enough to have 'convinced' you to have six more related thoughts, it doesn't mean that it will. It doesn't even mean that you believe that it will. Think about that for a moment. In fact, in a universe of infinite possibilities, the chance that the movie you have created will play out exactly as you have imagined it, is small. If this is low-grade worry it will result in a sense of 'dis-ease'. It will affect your judgement, making you risk-averse, scared or suspicious of change. In more extreme cases, as you imagine the stressful situation, your fight or flight will kick in, with all the physiological effects. Your stomach will tighten and your heart will race just as if that event was happening. Your brain does not distinguish between real or imagined experiences.

Once you start to recognise that your brain has hooked into a negative thought and the ANTs are on the march, you need to take charge and gently bring your focus back to the present moment. This is a quick exercise that will halt the spiral and give you the space to begin a new thought process that is more balanced and positive. It is the mnemonic of now, so it's really easy to remember.

Exercise 2.2: NOW

N – Notice: just glance around and notice one thing that you can see.

O – Observe: bring your close attention to the object that you have chosen; observe it in detail.

W – Wonder: bring a spirit of curiosity to the object you are observing. A negative thought cannot co-exist with positive engaged interest.

Remember that any sense works only in the present and will bring you back into the moment. This exercise, which focusses on observing, may work best for those who operate in a strongly visual way. Perhaps you love colours, imagine in 3D and always notice details. You may, however, be a person that instinctively functions in an aural way; you may feel most alive when playing music, listen more than you watch in a theatre and remember the words used in a conversation rather than the body language or facial expressions. If this is you, then focus in on a sound that you can hear instead of what you can see. Or you may be a person who naturally works kinaesthetically. Perhaps you love to dance, gesture often and tend to 'act out' a situation when you tell people what happened. If so, then move a part of your body when you do the exercise and concentrate on that.

It is finding the best way for you to bring your attention to the present. Or you could do the Image Breathing exercise, or others that we detail later. Remember, you don't want to battle with your brain; it isn't about conquering, it's about making friends. Bringing your attention to the present whenever you start to find your thoughts wandering to the past or future in a way that is not helpful will start to move you towards a greater appreciation and sense of wellbeing. We do not enjoy a life that is lived almost completely through memory and anticipation. This is important to remember, even if the remembering and the anticipation are largely positive; it's great to have things to look forward to, but excessive counting down the days to holidays can, for example, result in us missing out on a lot of life during the count. Our memories are precious and recalling them can give us great warmth and strength in later life, but living our life in highlights is no substitute for a deep appreciation of the simple and constant pleasures of our lives.

We've been asked many times why we have automatic thoughts. Well, most of the time they do a pretty good job. The fact that our brain can work automatically allows us to function in the way that we do. Imagine trying to do an activity such as playing football or driving if you had to give a single instruction for every physical action and thought required. We probably wouldn't even be able to tie up our football boots or get into the car! We are never going to rid our minds of automatic thoughts, nor would we want to, but it is possible to drastically reduce the tendency towards past-future negative spirals by reframing our beliefs, which we will focus on in Chapter 4, and by recognising the early signs and using a mindfulness exercise to bring the ANTs to rest.

As the ANTs come to rest, you may find that you reframe the way that you see the world around you. We live in a culture that is highly future-focussed. Many of us have, from an early age, the idea that what happens in the future is more important than what is happening to us now. If we do x now, then wealth, happiness, fulfilment and freedom will be the reward at some point in the future. The consumer society perpetuates this focus; we are encouraged to feel dissatisfied with our current lot in order that we purchase x and x to make us more satisfied in the future. While having goals (achievable goals) is positive and energising, it is a balance that needs to be watched. If we find that most of our 'doing', our 'present', is just a means to achieve a future goal (or avoid a future pain), then finding more joy in the present will certainly reinvigorate your life. It may well also reinvigorate your goals and your dreams.

Exercise 2.3: Past Noise

In your notebook, write down five situations that you have remembered over the last day or two. Often, we can manage to locate five from the last hour!

Write them out and just put a tick next to them if remembering them made you feel happy. We don't want to demolish those memories that give us strength and meaning. If, however, recalling the past was a negative experience, put a cross.

Continue to add to this list over the next week. Also start to notice when the Past Noise comes. Often it is weapon of self-sabotage at times when we most need to be focussed on something important.

Exercise 2.4: Future Noise

In your notebook, write down five situations that you have recently projected forwards to negative or worrying conclusions.

One at a time, go through the list and spend a minute re-imagining the situation playing out in a way that is advantageous to you or would bring you joy. It doesn't matter how unlikely that feels to you at the moment.

Negative Self-Talk

The second type of Noise, as we said, is Self-Talk and, of course, it is Negative Self-Talk that is damaging. This is the critic that knows all our foibles and fears and will sit on us at every opportunity. These thoughts might be connected to Past-Future Noise, for example blaming yourself for something that happened, or telling yourself that you could have done better. Of course it's essential to be able to reflect on our actions to sustain our moral compass and develop our abilities to course-correct, but we do not need to judge. Later in the book, we'll look at the transition from punishing ourselves to evaluating with a kindly but clinical eye.

Negative Self-Talk is also the million things we tell ourselves that we cannot do and, amazingly, we believe these little pests! Most of us have a fair few that we can bring to mind with little difficulty: 'I'm not the sort of person who can learn a language/do maths/change a plug/travel/learn IT skills/meditate.'

The list is endless. The Negative Self-Talk can, in fact, be really personal – 'I'm too fat/not clever/not funny/boring/I have no imagination', and so on. Can you imagine how outraged we would be if we heard someone voicing these to someone else!

Sometimes these thoughts come from something that was said to us once a long time ago in a specific situation; it's possible that this wasn't correct or was, at least, a harsh version of the truth, even at that time. For some people, it can be like living with a vicious gremlin in their head, always ready to leap out and attack.

But the great news is whatever the reason they are lurking in your mind they can be changed. As you learn to detach yourself from them through the mindfulness exercises and you learn to refocus the beliefs that have fed them over the years, they will gradually lose their power until they rarely come knocking.

Negative Self-Talk can also be related to fears and phobias. It may be that you have situations that frighten you. We all know that common fears can turn the most confident person into a jabbering wreck! Through the Mind Fitness process I have conquered my fear of heights and Andy can have a picnic in the summer without dancing round every time he hears a wasp!

Exercise 2.5: Forest of Self-Talk

As with some of our other exercises, this one requires a little use of imagination.

Start with a picture of you in the centre, drawn or a photograph – whichever works best for you.

Now draw a few trees around you and give each tree a speech bubble. Fill each bubble with a Negative Self-Talk statement.

If you have drawn your trees but can't think of any Negative Self-Talk to fill the speech bubbles, it's often useful to lower your defences by doing one of the mindfulness exercises to see what turns up. It's perfectly fine to build your forest gradually. Leave your picture to hand and, as and when you become aware of a stream of Self-Talk, fill in a bubble.

As you learn to notice the Noise, whether it be Past-Future or Negative Self-Talk, you become a more practised observer. You will know if your mind is giving you helpful pointers or ideas, or if it is delivering ANTs, which you can acknowledge and move on. You will be in control. Remember, the Noise is not the self. The self, freed from the Noise, is more content, more insightful and kinder. You will gradually be able to bring more and more of your full attention to the present moment. There are times in life where you will have experienced this by accident. A sunset that is so beautiful that you can see nothing else. A picture in a gallery that takes your breath away. Watching your child tie his shoelaces for the first time. The world you see will be more vivid and your connection with it will be a brighter, richer and deeper experience.

Pavlovian Triggers[3]

So why is it not as simple as just deciding to focus on the present? It's because of the way your mind works. The brain functions by looking into past events that seem similar to the current situation and using these to determine a 'solution' as well as a physiological response. The amygdala makes Pavlovian associations that we are not consciously aware of. A Pavlovian trigger is a conditioned response (in the same way that Pavlov's dogs were trained to respond unconsciously to various signals and commands.) Basically, it works in this way: if I 'see' this or 'hear' this, I will 'feel' this. Moments that spark an unconscious reaction are referred to as Pavlovian Triggers.

The reaction occurs without pause and with no decision and no understanding. In extreme cases, as with people suffering with post-traumatic stress disorder (PTSD) the amygdala enlarges as it becomes more metabolically reactive.[4] This is, of course, a million miles from the full analysis of advantages and disadvantages that would lead to good problem-solving and decision-making!

It could be, for example, that a piece of music was playing during a traumatic argument with an ex-partner. You may not even be aware of the memory, yet when you hear this piece of music your stomach will tighten and your mouth will become dry. It may even happen when you are standing in a crowded station and have not even noticed that the song is playing in the café that happens to spill out onto the concourse.

Smells are often very powerful triggers and ones that we are even less likely to be conscious of. Your new boss wears the same perfume as a controlling figure from your childhood – you just can't pinpoint why this compassionate and competent woman fills you with a sense of unease. You get the idea of how often this can occur. What is being activated is a pain pattern from your past.

Experts believe that the advent of social media has increased the triggering of the amygdala exponentially and this could be one of the many reasons for the current and ongoing dramatic increase of anxiety and stress-related illness.

You may be aware of a few of your triggers. If so it's worth starting a list in your notebook. As you work through the book and gain greater awareness, particularly when you begin identifying beliefs, you will become aware of more of them. As the triggers have led to cycles of repeat performances, they may well have become embodied in your sense of identity. 'I'm always so unlucky in … ' 'I am the kind of person who … ' 'I always choose partners that … ' 'It's me, isn't it' – so often a cry of unrecognised victimhood.

As with the Self-Talk, once you have acknowledged and accepted that they are there, the power of these triggers begins to wane. You will be able to use one of the mindfulness exercises, perhaps the short NOW exercise that we did earlier, to bring back your control as soon as you feel the first tightening of the stomach or whatever sign you recognise as approaching stress. The one that we have found most effective when we are leading training sessions is called Foxhole in My Mind. The first version of this exercise was 'invented' by President Truman in the Second World War. He was asked by his aides how it was that he was able to remain calm in the most stressful situations. He told them it was because he was able to take himself away from the situation whenever he needed to, that he had a foxhole in his mind.

Exercise 2.6: Foxhole in My Mind

Begin, as usual, by making sure that you are sitting comfortably. Take two breaths, breathing in through the nose and out through the mouth, now close your eyes.

The first stage of the exercise is to imagine a safe and beautiful place. It can be somewhere that you know from personal experience or a place that you have already 'seen', say from a book or film, or you can imagine somewhere completely new. As you think about the place, try to build in as much detail as possible. My Foxhole is an underwater Egyptian city. I imagine the details on the statues, the texture if I touch the rock, the temperature of the water. I can see, in detail, the fish that are swimming by me. I am usually floating, but I know what the sand feels like if my feet touch the ground. Once you have taken time to establish the place, imagine yourself moving through it. Notice how you feel in this safe and beautiful place.

The second stage of the exercise is to give yourself an Action Trigger (not to be confused with Pavlovian Triggers) to take yourself in and out of this space. Using a trigger will help you 'move' to the foxhole more quickly once your brain makes the automatic connection. My Action Trigger is two taps of my right hand on my left shoulder. I know people who use a finger click, a clap and even a raised eyebrow, a good one to choose if you want to do the exercise unobserved in busy meetings! Once you have chosen a simple action, try the exercise one more time, this time activating the experience with the trigger – staying in the space for say, one minute, and then using the trigger again to bring yourself out.

This is an exercise that takes a fair amount of time to do the first time as you build your picture, but, afterwards, is a quick and effective mindfulness exercise to be used when Pavlovian Triggers threaten to send you into a spiral of stress and panic. Try to make sure that each time you go into the exercise you put in something new, so that it always stays fresh. It is the equivalent of the sunset that takes your breath away. The more often you do the exercise, the quicker the physical levels of stress, such as increased heart beat and raised levels of the stress hormone cortisol, will come down as you trigger and go in. I have done it so often that I can usually beat my trigger. I barely have to lift my arm and I am under the sea!

Pleasure Triggers

Pleasure Triggers also work in a way that we are not consciously aware of. Dopamine is the chemical most often referred to as the 'pleasure neurotransmitter'.[5] The sensation of pleasure associated with eating chocolate, for example, comes from a release of dopamine. The chemical is released, however, not on eating but on our anticipation of eating! Many scientists believe that it is the neurological basis of addiction. We are not trivialising the seriousness of addiction and sometimes a package of support needs to be put in place, but certainly the programme can be used to change the mindset that sustains attachment to detrimental habitual behaviours. If you realise as you feel the rush, that your mind has taken you to future-focus, anticipating the piece of chocolate or the next cigarette, you may be able to bring your attention back to the present. This will reduce the urge and this, in turn, means that making changes in behaviour becomes easier with practice. If you need your dopamine hits there are more healthy ways of getting it, which we will look at in the chapter on positivity!

As you learn to observe your negative thoughts and to recognise triggers, they will, as we have said, lose their emotional charge. You will gradually feel more at peace with your mind; you will come to accept it and value it. It is a part of you and your wonder, not the enemy.

Exercise 2.7: Chapter Recap

A short practical exercise to reinforce what we have covered.

We'd like you to put in a few pinches of imagination to this chapter's recap. It will help you to remember what you have learned.

Draw a picture of the brain as you see it and put in little sticks coming out of it. At the end of each stick, write one piece of information about the brain that you know so far.

We have learned:

- ▶ You are not your brain
- ▶ How the brain works
- ▶ How to bring your attention to the present moment
- ▶ How Past-Future Noise can disturb you
- ▶ How Negative Self-Talk can disturb you
- ▶ How Pavlovian Triggers work
- ▶ How Pleasure Triggers work

Questions and Answers

> ▶ **My concern is that I have many Automatic Negative Thoughts (ANTs) that I'd like to deal with, but, along with that, I have a long-held need, superstitious belief almost, that if I don't think the worst about something that could happen in the future, it will tempt fate, making it likelier to occur.**
>
> We do hear these types of concerns during our workshops. A long-held belief can be entrenched and changing it will feel strange. Try to accept this and begin the process.

> ▶ **I have a lifetime of Negative Self-Talk. I am my harshest critic. It's absolutely entrenched. It's who I am and what I do. I really don't think I'm able to change that.**
>
> Many of us routinely condemn and damn ourselves. We speak to ourselves in ways that we could never even imagine treating others. There are many parts to making change, the first is acceptance. Another component is compassion, towards ourselves and to others. We can learn to be kinder to ourselves. That's not abdicating responsibility. It's simply accepting who we are, not damning ourselves for our errors. Steadily, we can create new neural pathways to cement that change. It takes time, practice and commitment, but it can be done.

Conclusion

You are not your brain but it is a vitally important part of you. And it is jaw-droppingly complex and awesome. The neocortex of the human brain contains 300 million pattern processors;[6] these are responsible for the storage and recall of patterns which result in all human thought. In fact, computer design principles for pattern processing were developed from the biological basis of pattern processing by the mammalian brain. How amazing is that?

It's easy to see why it is a very powerful enemy if it is working against us. But when we can harness that power, that capability, when we can make friends with our brain, we can realise our enormous potential. And when we have put ourselves in the strongest possible position, it becomes so much easier to make changes to the lives of other people and to become genuinely effective in the areas of your life that give you meaning.

3

You can change

Build new pathways in the brain that will take you to who you want to be

Neuroplasticity

As stated in the introduction, the accepted wisdom, until fairly recently, was that, once we reached adulthood, our brains and, therefore our personality and our identity had become fixed. Now we know, thanks to neuroscience, that we can remould our brain through the entirety of our life, and we know (and are continually learning more) about how the process works.[1] This means that we can change, and therefore choose, the way our mind thinks. We can change, and therefore choose, the way we experience the world. We can build new neural pathways in the brain that will take us towards the person that we want to be.

This magnificent ability is called neuroplasticity. I (BW) still remember my breath being taken away when I encountered the concept for the first time. In the 1990s, scientists recognised the ingenious ability of the central nervous system to repair itself after brain injury.[2] If these newly wired pathways were responsible for recovery, then it must mean that we continue to build new pathways through our adult life with all the ramifications for memory and new learning. Almost nothing outside of function related to survival is hard-wired.

We can change what we are thinking about, and the way we are thinking about it, and, by changing our thoughts, we can change our emotions and the patterns that seem to control our lives. We can change the way we feel about things that have always scared us. We can coach ourselves to be able to do the things we have long believed we can't. We can give a presentation confidently, overcome a fear of spiders, stride into a room and confidently hold our own at a party, if that's the thing we really want. If ever there was a magic wand that can cause real and lasting transformation, isn't it this?

It's true that it doesn't magic away the terrors and traumas of the external world but, if this is what comes into your mind, then just maybe you can remove the blocks that have always stopped you doing your bit to help. The spider still exists but the breeds that inhabit our skirting boards will not harm you. Go positively into the party for the room is yours.

Neuroplasticity is the process that allows the ABC Model[3] that we will look at in Chapter 4 to be effective at the deepest possible level. You can identify the beliefs that have stopped you from being the person you could be, challenge and change them. And you can do this because the process already exists, built into the workings of the brain.

How Neuroplasticity works

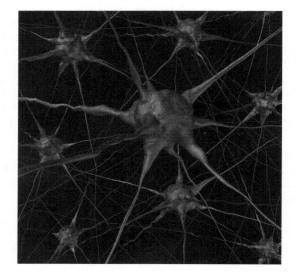

The brain contains billions of nerve cells called neurons that transmit signals to and from the brain. When the neurons connect, they create highways for the nerve signals (messages) to travel along. Basically, if a path is used often, the brain rebuilds itself to make the journey easier. If neurons are fired often at the same time as other neurons, then patterns form and pathways are created. For example, if you connect the smell of lavender with your great aunt Marge, it is likely that neurons relating to the image and the smell will fire together when you remember her, and a pathway will be formed. There is a phrase for it that we really like, 'neurons that fire together wire together'.[4]

Many pathways were created when we were children, formed by parental influence and youthful experience, and we continue to use them into adulthood. That's fine if the pathway is a positive belief or attitude. But there will be pathways formed by an unpleasant experience or a perceived trauma and these pathways will be making it hard for us to implement the changes that we know rationally would benefit us. This is because the brain will, under its own steam, take the most used, strongest pathway, the route of least resistance. These pathways might be telling us:

▶ I can't
▶ They should
▶ I must

We will look at these patterns of thinking later in the book.

We know now that we can build new neural pathways. When you learn something new or begin to adopt a new way of thinking about an issue, or about yourself or the wider world, your brain creates new neural pathways to facilitate this learning.

At first, your new pathway is fragile, a tentative track rather than a robust highway. But, as you use it more and more, it becomes strong and, if it is a pathway of a changed habit, eventually it takes over as the main thoroughfare, the route of least resistance.

An intellectual understanding will develop around the new habit; you know rationally that this works, this is helpful to you and will bring positive change to your life. Gradually, this becomes an emotional understanding; you feel it to be true, it fits the way you see yourself and it makes you happy.

How quickly and how deeply new habits embed depends on repetition and vigour – emotional commitment and investment. With these it generally it takes about six weeks. That's why our follow-up programme at the back of the book lasts this long.

It really does mean that there is no place for resignation and no need to settle for second best. Throughout time, nothing has gripped our imagination so much as the power to transform, from chrysalis into butterfly in nature, from base metal into gold in science and philosophy. Science has shown us now that transformation is a power that each and every one of us possesses.

Of course, there is only one magic wand and it is you. You can achieve real and lasting change if you want it enough.

Exercise 3.1: Commitment to Change

Make a list of five things that you wish you did or wish you didn't do.

Now give each a number of how much you want it on a scale of 1–10.

And, if you're sitting thinking 'I wish I had enough energy to do the things on my list' or 'I wish I didn't procrastinate and put off doing the things that I want', then put that on the list too! And give it a number.

Now, we don't know what you put on the list and some things might be unachievable. But we can certainly achieve extraordinary things. It just takes practice. It is the only effective method so far found. Interestingly though, struggle within the practice is good; it can speed up the process. Don't worry if it sometimes feels hard.

The magnitude of what can be achieved by CBT (using Neuroplasticity) in the treatment of long-term complex disorders is extraordinary. Therapies can be effective with people with the most profound PTSD,[5] for example soldiers returning from active service who have experienced traumas most of us would find hard to imagine. It is used every day in clinics around the world to treat depression, personality disorders and psychosis. It is also used to address addictions and phobias. And it works.

How easy is it to change?

What does it take to make it work? As we've said, it takes practice and commitment. You have to want to change. What it doesn't take is time. At least, not the kind of time that has to be fitted into an already bulging schedule. The title of this book is *Unlock You*, and we genuinely believe that, once you have embedded all the techniques into your daily life, all it will take is five minutes at the beginning and end of each day to do active development work, to make sure you keep moving in the right direction. What it does take is the kind of time that you have plenty of because your brain and you are together 24/7.

At the beginning it will be a conscious process. You will become aware that the moments when your brain is less 'occupied', for example standing in a crowded train, waiting in a supermarket queue, are the times when you are likely to trundle off into the list of things you haven't done and let the ANTs make mush of your resolutions. Gradually, you will come to fill these 'gaps' with positive thoughts, positive self-talk and affirmations – all the things that get you stepping off the train in a better state than when you got on.

As time passes, you will become less and less aware of being on ANT repulsion duty. Your new positive thoughts will be a sufficient guard for any lurking fears or worries. The new pathways will be those most used, the routes of least resistance.

Why do you want to change? Who do you want to be?

Before we look, in the next chapter, at identifying beliefs, challenging and changing them, using the wonderful world of neuroplasticity, let's step back for a minute and ask the big question. 'Who do you want to be?' Now that we know we can change our brain in ways that will change our thoughts, emotions and values – essentially our identity, our personality – which is the you that you want to be?

Some of you will never have thought about it. And it's likely that the way we think about our goals and ambitions will have become as much of a habit, a neural pathway, as anything else. We probably have something that we reel off at the odd social occasion if someone asks us:

'I'm working my way to being a partner in the firm.'

'Of course, I'd rather be my own boss.'

'I come from a big family, so I'd like to have lots of kids.'

'I'd like to go back into acting one day.'

And each time we say this, we consolidate a vision of ourselves that we may not have even considered, let alone challenged for years. If you have one of these 'visions', now is the time to give it a shake and see if it's still fit for purpose. Is that what you really want for yourself? Is that the *you* you'd like to be?

Exercise 3.2: Successful You

Imagine yourself a little distance into the future, when you have made changes to your beliefs, your mind, your life.

You are going to congratulate this future you on five successes – they can be little or big.

Write them down:

1 _____

2 _____

3 _____

4 _____

5 _____

And now congratulate yourself for each one of them. Say it out loud.

Adaptive Behaviour

Science also shows us that we can prepare our brain to be disposed to build new habits and behaviour by making continual changes. It's called Adaptive Behaviour. A brain that is used to constant change, however small, builds new pathways more easily.

To use the ABC Model to challenge and change your beliefs, and to move from non-constructive to constructive tendencies or habits, is Adaptive Behaviour. The more you can build change into your life, the easier this will be to do.

There is also evidence that a brain that is used to small changes copes much more effectively with a sudden big change or crisis.

We are, most of us, creatures of habit. We like to put the tea in before the milk or the milk in before the tea. We'll tie our shoes right and then left or left and then right. We have our ways, our routes. There are probably roads close to where you live that you have never travelled. In our training sessions, we ask people to take their watches or bracelets off and put them on the other wrist. You'd be amazed at how much discomfort this can cause. Try it now if you are wearing one. We've had numerous people say, 'But I don't feel like me!' And anybody who has kicked a habit such as smoking will know that one of the most powerful sensations that has to be overcome is the feeling that you have lost or given up something that made you *you*, perhaps even lost a part of 'yourself'.

That the method of reducing the habit-led disorientation is to do more of the same (for example more of the not smoking) feels counterintuitive. There can be a very strong sense of unease or restlessness. Then when the pathway becomes strong you feel settled again, comfortable with your brain, comfortable in your skin. Not that you will be the same you, but perhaps a happier, more contented you, if you have changed a negative habit or belief for one that is more positive. It is a step along the journey of merging your habitual behaviour with your meaning and goals. A step towards becoming the person that you want to be.

If making constant small changes is a way of preparing our brains to be more 'plastic', it's important that it's a way of life that we commit to. And, actually, most people report that it makes them feel younger, more adventurous, more alive. Even the act of actively looking for things you want to change may give us an enticing sense of freedom, of shaking off shackles.

Exercise 3.3: Small Things You Can Change Right Now!

Part 1

Write three small things that you can change right now!

1 _____

2 _____

3 _____

Part 2

Spend a day actively looking for things you can change and add them to the list you have started above. It's only when there's a stack of things staring up at you that you realise just how many of the same things you do every day!

Adaptive Behaviour and Dementia Prevention

There's one more really good reason to start making small and constant changes. There is now some really solid research linking Adaptive Behaviour with dementia prevention.

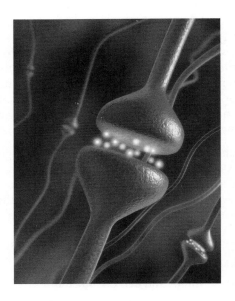

Scientists believe that what causes Alzheimer's is a build-up of beta-amyloids at synapses, eventually causing them to break down.[6] Synapses are where neurons meet or nearly meet allowing electrical and chemical signals to pass between them, allowing us to think, feel and remember. Beta-amyloids are protein fragments that clump into plaques, leading to nerve cell death. Key features of Alzheimer's are wholesale loss of synapses and a parallel deterioration of brain function, notably in the ability to remember.

But if you are constantly learning, doing new things and meeting new people, there will be new synapses being formed. This bank of functioning synapses is called Cognitive Reserve. You will not need to rely only on those connections that are breaking down.

It seems to be especially effective if the new experiences are rich and involve emotions as well as thoughts. It is important to note that we are talking about new learning. It's not enough to do crossword puzzles; these are retrieving old information and not about new learning, new experience. If we are looking to develop our Mind Fitness, then building Cognitive Reserve should be part of that plan. If we hit the difficult age and we're Mind Fit, if we have deeply embedded positive techniques, it puts us into a much stronger position to cope with the changes in brain function.

Exercise 3.4: Chapter Recap

Write, in one sentence, what Neuroplasticity is. (Only use the science and the jargon if you think it's fun!)

Write out a couple of the benefits of Adaptive Behaviour.

Identify someone in your circle that you think is particularly adaptive to change.

Questions and Answers

▶ **Having created new neural pathways and established new beliefs and behaviours, how easy is it to go back to our old ways?**

The brain is super-efficient. Thoughts are transmitted along the most used neural pathways so that change requires us to consciously create new pathways and deliberately think in those ways. Over time, the old pathways reduce and the new become the norm. But, of course, old pathways can be re-established. Be vigilant and allow time for conscious change.

▶ **I hate change. Always have. I'm a creature of habit and find great comfort in continuity. Why do I need to be adaptive?**

Adaptive Behaviour is about embracing change. Change is the one and only certainty in life, but fear of change is part of the human condition. Learning to become more adaptive reduces our self-triggered anxiety born out of perceived threat by demystifying change and challenging our demands for comfort. Adaptability is needed to develop and grow. In time, you may even learn to enjoy the prospect and process of change.

Conclusion

Once or twice in training sessions we've had people say 'Well this is marvellous, what's the catch?' There isn't a catch, but there is one aspect of Neuroplasticity that perhaps should give us pause for thought. It leads us to believe that there are pressing reasons for us to rewire our brains and change our behaviours that are bigger than our individual ambitions and even our meaning. We know now that everything we think, do and experience affects our brain on a chemical, structural and functional level. We and our brains are constantly shaped by the world around us. This means that we have the enormous potential of positively affecting huge numbers of other people by the things we say and do. That, of course, is brilliant. But the opposite is also true.

While positive relational experiences, the way we react with others in a million ways, will help them be strong, confident and happy, negative relational experiences will have the opposite detrimental effect. Understanding how the brain works places a new responsibility on us all. It's no longer enough that we didn't *mean* to cause offence or hurt. If the other person has experienced that hurt or offence, the damage has been done. And in today's world we don't even have to be there, it can be a message that we sent online or posted on social media.

It's just another reason to make sure that you use this book to become calm, confident and happy. The benefit of these changes will be felt by those you love and a host of other people with whom you interact in your daily life.

And just think, the three chapters that you have already read, the exercises you have already done and the *you* that you have imagined, will already have changed your brain. You have already begun to build the brain you want.

4

Change your response

How to change the way that you respond to everything that happens

This is the chapter that explains the ABC Model.[1] This is where you learn to change the way that you respond to the troublesome things that happen in your life. It is, quite simply, a life changer.

Both Rational Emotive Behavioural Therapy (REBT) and its better-known cousin Cognitive Behavioural Therapy (CBT) are used throughout the world to treat anxiety, depression, addiction, post-traumatic stress disorder (PTSD) and a wide variety of personality disorders. Ours is a coaching model focussing on performance and self-improvement rather than the clinical version of the process.

A key aspect of both REBT and CBT is that they are time-limited. This means that you sign up for a short period, during which you learn how to be your own coach and build new patterns of behaviour into your daily routines. If, in the future, a problem arises, as it almost certainly will, you will know how to tackle it.

The philosophies behind REBT are ancient, dating back to Epictetus in the first century. He was a Stoic philosopher, quoted as saying, 'Men are disturbed, not by things, but by the view they take of them.' In other words, it's not so much what happens to you but the way you respond that matters. A follower of Epictetus, the Roman Emperor Marcus Aurelius, said, 'Very little is needed to make a happy life; it is all within yourself, in your way of thinking.' Hundreds of years later, the great bard William Shakespeare writes in Hamlet, 'There is nothing either good or bad but thinking makes it so.'

REBT and CBT

Modern psychotherapy reinvented this ancient thinking. In the mid 1950s, Albert Ellis, a New York based psychologist, developed REBT to help people to change their irrational thinking and behaviour by highlighting and challenging their unhelpful, rigid beliefs.

Aaron T. Beck, the creator of CBT, followed the same basic model, but focussed on cognitive distortions which are unhelpful types of thinking.

The REBT-based ABC Model is at the heart of this book and the Mind Fitness process. Once you learn to examine your deep-rooted beliefs and attitudes using this, everything changes. You will no longer be vulnerable to the storms of other people. You will stop giving consent to feeling inferior and you will be in control of your emotions. Almost everything else in the book supports this process of change.

The ABC Model

The ABC Model enables the reframing of issues that cause emotional disturbance. In other words it gets to the root of why we get disturbed, why we get upset.

ABC is an acronym:

A – Activating event or Adversity

B – Belief/s you hold about the Activating event or Adversity

C – Consequence of having the Belief about the Activating event or Adversity

Read through that a couple of times. It's actually a lot simpler than it may at first seem. The best way to illustrate it is to go through the model using a fairly trivial example of day-to-day adversity that most of us experience at some time or other.

You know the sort of day you can have when everything seems to be conspiring against you? I don't mean terrible things, just a succession of annoying situations that can cause us to feel stressed and agitated. It's very easy for a situation that is by nature relatively trivial to become something that we manage to lose perspective of. We allow it to become a big issue. It upsets us, creating anxiety. That stresses us and results in a loss of temper or a lack of control of our emotions. We may snap at someone, even punch an inanimate object. Possibly swear loudly and liberally! You know the kind of day we're referring to. We've all been there.

Let's give a specific situation. You'd like to get to work earlier than usual for an important meeting. You're late leaving the house because the document you need for the meeting wasn't in your bag. You search the house, trying to locate it and waste far too much time. You think you may have left it at work, but you can't be sure. It's ok, you'll print off another copy when you get in, although your plan was to prepare during the journey in. Why do you always leave things to the last minute?

Now you're running really late. You race out of the house and sprint to the bus stop. It starts raining and you realise that you've forgotten your umbrella. You arrive at the stop just as your bus is heading off into the distance. There's a 20-minute wait for the next bus and the indicator is showing a delay. You know that you'll be late for the meeting. You won't have time now to print off the document when you get in and you'll have to busk it. That, on top of turning up late and drenched, will not show you in a good light. You're really soaked now and getting colder. You're also becoming seriously stressed. You're berating yourself for being so stupid. You *had* to be at the meeting on time and up to speed with the supporting information. What an idiot you are for not preparing everything the night before. Why didn't you at least read the document through when you had the chance last night, just in case there was a problem? Now you'll have to take the walk of shame, arriving late at the meeting.

Your colleagues will think you're incompetent and unprofessional. This is bound to affect your chances of promotion. It's game over now. You don't actually merit having a good job. It wouldn't surprise you if they began a process to force you out.

Does that seem familiar? Can you recall a situation when you made an already unfortunate situation so much worse?

Let's put this event into the ABC Model:

A - Activating Event or Adversity

In other words, the thing that happens. The situation you find yourself in.

Being late for an important meeting through a wholly avoidable, self-inflicted delay.

Now, I'm going to jump straight to **C – Consequences**. That's because it's something we do without realising. It's called A to C thinking. This thing happened and it **made** me feel like this and **made** me do this.

So, what are the Consequences of this situation? A consequence has several elements.

1 Emotional – the emotions we feel about the situation
2 Action tendency – this is what we feel like doing even if we don't act on it
3 Behavioural – the behaviour we display – how we react
4 Physiological – the physical results (symptoms)

C - The Consequences of our story would look something like this:

Emotional

Clearly, you feel a strong sense of anxiety. And anger. You're angry that you've been so stupid, that you've behaved irresponsibly, counter to your usually higher standards. You also feel a sense of shame for letting down your personal rules on professionalism and you're pre-empting the shame you'll undoubtedly feel when you eventually arrive late and underprepared at the meeting.

Action Tendency

You want just to go home and call in sick. It wouldn't be a total lie – you're feeling pretty bad.

Behavioural

The anger has provoked an aggressive attitude. Swearing under your breath. Mostly damning yourself but, quite possibly, a mistimed comment from someone at the bus stop could be met by a less than friendly response at this stage.

Physiological

Your symptoms include racing heart, not just from the exertion of the journey to the bus stop, but because your Fight and Flight Stress Response has kicked in. You're upset and you're dreading the meeting, so your stomach is turning. You're flushed, again not just because you've run for the bus, but because of that stress response. Take a moment to think of a time when you've felt and exhibited at least some of these symptoms.

You're stressed, angry, wet and dejected at the bus stop. You wait impatiently for a bus that may arrive late, making the situation and your stress levels worse as every minute ticks by. You would probably sum up the situation thus:

- ▶ I missed my bus because I didn't prepare as I should have and now I'm going to be late for an important meeting.
- ▶ I'm now stressed, angry, upset and when I mess up in the meeting, I'm bound to lose my job.

There's an important part of this situation missing. Here's how we can check what that is. We'll use something called the 100 person rule.

100 Person Rule

If 100 people were in exactly the same situation that you found yourself in, would they all react in the same way? Would everyone get stressed? Would everyone beat themselves up and condemn themselves? Would everyone envisage the worst outcome, regard their colleagues as hostile and uncaring? Think of 100 people in any situation, say 100 recent divorcees. You wouldn't expect them all to be depressed. Some may be ecstatic, or at least see it as an opportunity to move on. Each person has a unique take in any given situation.

Something is missing from our A to C view of the scenario. It is the Belief. It's the Beliefs that we hold that govern our response to the Adversity and so govern our response to any situation.

B - Beliefs

Let's take a look at Beliefs. The first thing to make clear is that we want to challenge the irrational Beliefs that are leading to unhelpful emotions or behaviours. It's not about overturning your value system or spiritual beliefs. The process works equally well for people with or without what might be considered 'faith'.

The Beliefs to which we refer are based around our attitudes, the meaning we place on the things in our lives. Our Beliefs are drawn from the personal rules that we hold. As we've said before some of these were gained in childhood so are long held and deeply ingrained. They are our truths and they guide us and form the basis of who we think we are.

The Beliefs, these personal truths and values, can help us to be remarkable and to do amazing things. They allow us to be kind, thoughtful, compassionate and selfless. Our Beliefs enable us to uphold personally important values such as generosity, honesty or integrity. Clearly, our Beliefs can be very positive, empowering and beneficial. But what happens when they're not?

For example what if we have carried, possibly from childhood, a Belief that we are fundamentally stupid? In fact, plenty of us carry this or a version of this negative Belief. We believe that we can't possibly succeed because we're not clever enough to do so. It's likely that such a limiting Belief will lead to a lifetime of missed opportunities. The Beliefs that we hold, our truths, have a fundamental influence on the way we live, on our relationships, our successes and our ultimate happiness.

The word belief belies a complexity of components that can serve us well or trip us up. Our beliefs can limit our opportunities and make us get in our own way. They determine the way that we view ourselves, others and the wider world.

A Belief can be:

Unusual or Commonplace

An unusual belief could be that as I love a drink, I don't trust anyone who doesn't. A commonplace belief might be that people must thank me for holding a door open for them. If they don't show me that common courtesy and sail straight through without acknowledging me in any way, it annoys me, and I react negatively.

True or False

A true belief is that the sun will rise tomorrow (it depends on universal rather than man-made laws).

A false belief is that we must always appear happy, that despite everything, we must always be cheerful.

Realistic or Unrealistic

A realistic belief could be that not everyone likes me. There will always be people who will be indifferent.

An unrealistic belief is that absolutely everyone, without exception, hates me.

Rigid or Flexible

A rigid belief could also be described as absolutist or dogmatic. This *must* happen. I *have* to be perfect when I present to the board.

A flexible belief is about preferences. I would prefer to be perfect when I present to the board, but I accept that excellence is the most I can achieve.

Helpful or Unhelpful

Helpful beliefs are those that are beneficial to you – I understand that I cannot possibly be excellent in everything I do all of the time, but I can try my best and aim to be the best I can be.

Unhelpful beliefs tend to fit in around the rigid, unrealistic or false. I must be perfect 100 per cent of the time, and failure to comply with this demand makes me a wholly bad person.

Exercise 4.1: Example Beliefs

Let's have a quick practice at identifying these. You can use your own beliefs, but if in any section you cannot think of one for you, think of a close friend and see if you can select one for him or her.

A commonplace belief

An unusual belief

A true belief

A false belief

A realistic belief

An unrealistic belief

A rigid belief

A flexible belief

A helpful belief

An unhelpful belief

The beliefs that we hold are formed of our attitudes (how things should or must be), our expectations (how we must behave, how others must behave or how the world must treat us) and our personal rules (our own hard-wired laws of the universe that we hold and defend as though they were real laws). We apply these rules doggedly when judging ourselves (often harshly), others and the world.

Many of us feel that our beliefs make us who we are, from our disposition or nature to our political stance or lack of. It's because our beliefs are so closely aligned to our sense of identity that we will often defend them even if they are wholly unhelpful. We can only say that the benefits you will reap by taking the road to reframing them will give you a renewed sense of self that is far stronger and more authentic.

Back to the situation

Let's now look again at our scenario – we're running late, we've missed the bus and we now have the spectre of not arriving at our important meeting on time. Everything seems to be conspiring against us!

Remember we said that, if 100 people were placed in an identical situation, each person would have a different view. That's how we can discount the A to C scenario that we originally used, the assumption that the activating event leads directly to the consequences. If it did we would all react the same. It doesn't! It's the beliefs that we hold that determine the consequences.

Let's now add the B for Beliefs into the ABC Model.

A – A Being late for an important meeting through an avoidable, self-inflicted delay.

B – Belief/s held about the activating event or adversity (the situation).

I *must* never be late

It is *awful* and totally unacceptable to be late

I *can't bear* being seen negatively by my colleagues

I am totally stupid. It proves what an idiot I am

C – Consequence of the activating event?

Emotional – Anxiety, anger, shame

Action tendency – To run away

Behavioural – Aggression, swearing

Physiological – Heart racing, stomach churning, flushed, fighting back tears

This illustration demonstrates that it isn't the event itself that causes the unpleasant consequences, but the unhelpful, rigid and irrational beliefs that we hold. It is these that disturb us. Let's spend a moment looking at the beliefs that are tripping us up.

1 I *must* never be late. This belief is a rigid, dogmatic, all or nothing personal rule applied as if it was a law. But how rational or reasonable is it to hold such a rigid demand about something that we cannot always control? Sure, in this scenario, we could have left home earlier, so we can

take some responsibility for our predicament. But to never ever be late? Is that feasible? Achievable? What is bound to happen at some point? We're going to be late through no fault of our own and this rigid belief will result in our experiencing the inevitable emotional disturbance. We're lining ourselves up for a fall. It's not a matter of if, but when.

2   It is *awful* and totally unacceptable to be late. Of course, being late for anything is not ideal. It can be annoying for others who are kept waiting and can be seen as rudeness. Is it really, truly *awful* though? We'll look in more detail at our tendency to 'awfulise' or 'catastrophise' in Chapter 6.

3   I *cannot bear* to be seen negatively by my colleagues. 'I cannot bear it' or 'I cannot stand it' are examples of low frustration tolerance which we will look at in Chapter 6. Although the experience is highly unpleasant you can bear it. (We all can bear far more than we instinctively think.)

4   I am totally stupid. It proves what an idiot I am. One minor transgression and you're liable to damn yourself as being totally stupid? All of us can do less than perfect things from time to time. That's all part of being human. But totally stupid? That's another huge leap of logic. Does it prove you're an idiot? Are you actually an idiot? No!

We can now begin to understand how easy it has been to turn an unfortunate, though relatively trivial, situation into an awful one. It hasn't been the situation itself that has caused us the upset. It's the beliefs we hold about the situation.

This knowledge is power! We can change the way we think and powerfully and positively alter the consequences of difficult situations. We can use the ABC Model as a mechanism to evaluate a situation, identify our irrational beliefs and adopt the process to change to a more flexible, realistic alternative. In terms of our journey towards confidence and happiness and achieving the potential that is buried inside us, this is gold!

Irrational Beliefs

Before we look closely at the process of change, we should spend a moment understanding more about irrational beliefs.

Irrational Beliefs are:

▶ Rigid or extreme
▶ Inconsistent with reality
▶ Illogical
▶ Unhelpful to us in pursuing our goals

Exercise 4.2: Identify Those Irrational Beliefs

Using the story example, we are now more easily able to identify the types of irrational beliefs from these lists. So, from the four beliefs that we identified in our being late story, allocate the types of irrational belief to each statement that you think is applicable.

Types of Irrational Beliefs:

▶ Demands

▶ Awfulising

▶ Low frustration tolerance

▶ Self/other/life depreciating

Jot down a note by each to say why:

1 I must never be late

2 It is awful and totally unacceptable to be late

3 I cannot bear being thought of negatively by my colleagues

4 I am totally stupid; it proves what an idiot I am

Disputing

With your new-found knowledge, you'll get increasingly used to identifying your own and other people's irrational, unhelpful beliefs. This self/other awareness is a major step in changing the unhelpful ways you think, feel and behave. To do this and effect lasting change, we'll add another letter to the ABC Model. **D – Disputing.**

The purpose of the Disputing process is to recognise and then test for the validity of your beliefs that may be influencing situations. At the outset, you'll probably find it easiest to use the ABCD process in a fairly formal way, writing each step down, but in no time you'll be able to run through the process in your head to determine a more helpful viewpoint.

There are four disputing questions to ask yourself regarding a belief you hold. Let's use as an example the belief that 'I must always be perfect 100 per cent of the time in everything I do'.

▶ **Is it true?**
    Is your belief true? No. The use of the word *must* tells us that this statement is a rigid demand. Is perfection possible? And having to *always*

be perfect? This is an irrational perfectionist-based belief that could cause upset to yourself and possibly others. We'll have a look at perfectionism in more detail in Chapter 6.

▶ **Is it logical?**
Is it logical to expect that because you demand perfection 100 per cent of the time, this will happen? Does it make sense? No. What happens when inevitably it doesn't? How does that make you feel and behave?

▶ **Is it helpful? It is sometimes easier to think 'How does it help me?'**
It's likely that holding this belief is not helpful. It can create the tendency to procrastinate, to put off the task for fear of not living up to your irrational demand. That can lead to real and damaging feelings of failure. You're setting yourself up to fail. It's a self-defeating strategy. It may also have wider implications if you demand perfection of others.

▶ **Would you teach the belief to others?**
Based on the answers to the previous two questions, it's highly unlikely that you would recommend such a belief to others, such as friends or perhaps your children. This we find is the killer question. When coaching using the ABCD Model, this is the point where even the longest held and most guarded belief is finally questioned. The process of change can now begin.

The process of change – changing Demands to Preferences

We saw in Chapter 3 that, thanks to Neuroplasticity, we're able to change the way we feel, think and behave if we really want to. We can change even the things we have held most dear, beliefs and attitudes that we have long assumed to be part of our character. Many times on our courses we've been told, 'Well of course I've always been a worrier and my mother was a worrier. I didn't stand a chance!' Worry is not an inherited trait! If you'd prefer not to consider yourself a congenital 'worrier', then you have the ability to be something else. You have the power to change.

We know that rigid demands are unhelpful, so if we are seriously intending to make changes these need to be reframed. Is there an alternative to a demand? There is. A preference! Why is a preference better? Because a demand gives us just one option. A demand is dogmatic, rigid. I must.

They should. We have to. You either do or don't meet the terms of a demand. A preference, however, gives two or more options.

What do we mean by a preference in this context? We can express a preference as: 'I would *prefer* to always produce perfect work, *but* I accept that perfection is impossible and so striving for excellence, which is achievable, makes far more sense. In future that's what I'll aim for.'

When I (BW) first began working with the ABC Model it was this that I found most liberating. I worked hard to coach myself into thinking of preferences rather than demands and it really does make the world seem a different place. For a few months I had to do it consciously. When a difficult situation arose, I talked myself through the process:

▶ *I would prefer* that the arts centre where my group of disabled actors rehearse had not used the set of their play to make into Santa's Grotto *but* I accept that this has happened and we can probably come to a compromise.

▶ *I would prefer* that I could still drive (I have glaucoma) *but* I accept that this is not possible and there's a bus stop outside my house.

I've done it for so long that it's now my go-to response, my most used pathway. I literally think in terms of preferences, and the reduction in stress is huge. I think it's also made me appreciate other people more, and probably myself too. If I catch myself thinking a rigid demand, I know I must be tired and make sure I find the time to rest.

Exercise 4.3: Preferences

Write out three demands that you hold or have held in the past. Now change them into preferences. 'I would prefer that ... but ... .'

1

2

3

ABC Thinking

This is the exciting bit. We're ready now to start using the ABC Model. Try to be as honest as you can when you are identifying your beliefs and the issues that are worrying you.

Exercise 4.4: Using the ABC Model

We're going to map out the first stage of the ABC process, identifying a Belief about an Activating Event and the resulting Consequence, including the emotion, behaviour and physiological symptom.

Take a few minutes to think of an issue or problem that you're currently having. It may be an ongoing adversity or a current worry or challenge.

A – Adversity. What is the problem or issue? Capture it as succinctly as possible.

B – Belief. What is or are the beliefs that you hold about the A? Is the belief rigid? A demand? Can you identify a personal rule? Remember must, have to, need to.

C – Consequence.

Emotional – notice how it makes you feel. We'll look in detail at emotions and the ways to address Unhealthy Negative Emotions in Chapter 11.

Action Tendency – what does it make you want to do?

Behavioural – note your behaviour regarding the adversity.

Physiological (symptoms) – headache? Raised heartrate?

Let's dispute the Belief that you have selected:

▶ Is it true?

▶ Is it logical?

▶ Is it helpful?

▶ Would you teach this belief to others?

How could you reframe the belief so that it is more helpful? For example, changing it to a preference if it is based around a rigid demand.

If you did this, what might your new, more helpful belief look like?

Write it down. (We always find it helpful to say it out loud.)

Now close your eyes and imagine how this new more helpful belief might change the consequences.

Remember the Activating event or Adversity is still the same – it is the way that you respond to this that changes.

At the end of this chapter is a simple Disputing Form to use when in the future you challenge unhelpful beliefs. If you don't use it before, you will use this as part of the six-week follow-up programme at the back of the book.

Questions and Answers

▶ **If I move from my rigid beliefs to preferences won't I become less effective?**

You can uphold extremely high standards and rigorous aspirations with flexible, realistic beliefs and achievable goals. We can have a preference for the highest standards in others, but we cannot demand them as we do not have full control over other people. We can disturb ourselves significantly by making demands of ourselves and others that simply will never be met.

▶ **What happens if a truly awful event occurs? How does the ABC Model help with that?**

Sadly, dreadful things do happen. REBT from which the ABC Model derives is very effective for helping people who have experienced trauma. As we've said, PTSD is treated widely through the use of cognitive therapies. It's not about trying to change the event, it's about how we view it. People who experience trauma may go on to suffer consequences such as feelings of guilt or anger. REBT and the ABC Model are very effective in helping people to reframe their view of the trauma in order to enhance the healing process.

Conclusion

Learning the ABC Model and integrating it into your daily life and habitual mental process is a key part of Mind Fitness. When you are consciously determining how you respond to a situation and choosing a response that benefits rather than disturbs or damages you, you regain an enormous amount of control over your life.

We're not saying that life will instantly become easy and filled with joy; this isn't fantasy land. But you'll be able to reduce the unnecessary worry about what will or might happen, and to manage your emotions in a way that minimises upset and conflict. Stopping our unhelpful beliefs tripping us up is a big step in the journey towards a you that is calmer, happier and significantly more able to cope with the challenges of life.

Disputing Form

Use this formula to test your Beliefs

The Activating Event or Adversity:

Your Belief about the Activating Event or Adversity:

Dispute that Belief

Is your Belief true?
Realistic? Consistent with reality? Where's your evidence to support your Belief?

Is your Belief logical?
Because you want something to happen, it **MUST**?

Is your Belief helpful?
Does the belief help or hinder you?

Would you teach your Belief to others?

Using the ABC Model, reframe your Belief so that it is a flexible preference, non-awfulising and High Frustration Tolerant.

Your new reframed Belief:

Dispute your new reframed Belief

Is your Belief true?
Realistic? Consistent with reality? Where's your evidence to support your Belief?

Is your Belief logical?
Because you want something to happen, it MUST?

Is your Belief helpful?
Does the belief help or hinder you?

Would you teach your Belief to others?

5

Set good goals

How to set goals that are in line with your new positive beliefs and keep to them

Preparing to set your goals

Setting your goals should be something that gives you a bit of a tingle. I always get the same feeling of 'lighting up' that I got as a child when I was taken to the Pic 'n Mix sweet counter and handed the empty bag.

It's good to make it a big deal. Put a couple of inspiring quotes on the table. Buy a bottle of wine or quality fizzy water. Only one glass of the wine though, you want to be fully present.

It's amazing how many people don't set goals for themselves at all or, if they do, give so little thought to it that it might be better if they hadn't. We spend ages choosing a holiday destination because we don't want to waste two weeks, yet waste years by setting goals and targets that mean little or nothing to us, and that aren't going to make us happy.

Others pick totally unobtainable targets, perhaps because, in a strange way, it lets them off the hook from going all-out to achieve them. It's never going to happen anyway, so what's the point?

And, for many people, as we mentioned in Chapter 3, the 'goals' they have in their mind, shaping their destiny, are goals they selected years ago. If you are a person who has always had a single burning passion or ambition, a vocation, then perhaps the goal you set 10 or 20 years ago is still entirely relevant. It still gives you the tingle and makes you feel alive. For most people, that won't be the case. If you have a different partner, a different house, a different job, then it is likely that you also need different goals.

Anyone who has had children knows that, suddenly, all goals are bundled up into a sack and scattered. Some land close by but others get taken off by the wind or the stream of daily life. This is not because you are 'forgetting your dreams' or 'burying your hopes', it's simply that you have a new list of priorities. You wouldn't change it for the world.

It's important to identify the goals you have *now* and to tie them in closely with the most helpful of your beliefs and with your meaning.

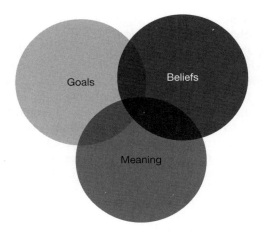

Before we start, have a glance at the list of 'wants' you made in your note-book when you were reading Chapter 3. You made a note of how much you wanted them. How would you evaluate them now? Does the thought of achieving them make you excited? Do they have the tingle factor?

It's likely that some will and some won't. I mean, that's two chapters ago and a lot can happen in that time once you start understanding your incredible brain!

It's probably time to throw a few new goals and ambitions into the mix. To think about what you *really* want. What do you really want to do? Who do you really want to *be*? It's also worth mentioning that not all goals that you set need to be huge or life-changing.

Many years ago, I (AB) worked in the theatre and, after several years of sporadic low-paid work, I landed a long contract with a West End show. A regular pay packet meant that I could set some longer-term goals. I discovered the pleasure of setting myself a goal of saving a small amount of money every week. To set and stick to it and see the savings balance increase modestly each week was incredibly motivating and pleasurable. It was an early lesson in how setting achievable goals can bring positive difference and improve life quality.

Perhaps, though, you are struggling to find something you truly feel would fire you up. It's not unusual for people to lose touch with even the sense of their hopes and their dreams. There can be a myriad of reasons – cynicism has set in or perhaps you have had a long-term struggle that has drained you of all but the need to survive. Some give up their goals willingly to assist another person, without realising that this has, in itself, become a determining goal.

For whatever reasons, there are a significant number of people who we have worked with who have 'confessed' that they don't know what they are passionate about. If this is you, then your first goal is to find something. To actively search, with hope and curiosity, until you find something about which you care deeply. It usually doesn't take very long. I (BW) have a friend who, after the end of a long relationship, went looking for her 'mojo'. She began evening classes in acting, salsa and quantum mechanics. She started volunteering at her local hospice. Almost everyone thought she was seeking a new partner, but she said she was looking for her flame. She rather wonderfully found both in that she re-met an old flame who is now a new flame, supporting her through a course in cosmology.

Setting your goals

We're going to do a quick mindfulness-based exercise to bring you to the moment and place you in the best possible state to set your goals.

Exercise 5.1: Heart of the Matter

Begin by getting yourself comfortable on a chair, arms on your knees or in your lap and feet flat on the floor. For a moment, experience the sensation of any part of your body that is in contact with the chair or with the floor, and perhaps with any clothes that you are wearing. Take two deep breaths to centre yourself, then close your eyes.

From an awareness of your breath, move to an awareness of your heart. Feel where it is placed and sense its relationship with the breath and the rest of the body. Imagine your heart in whatever way you feel comfortable, a working organ or a Disney red velvet shape; any picture that feels right to you.

While focussing on the image of your heart, take four breaths. Let any thoughts that come into your mind while you do the exercise gently drift away.

Now see if you can imagine a physical tingling sensation that begins at your fingertips and moves up through your arms. When it reaches your shoulders and your whole arms are tingling, release the energy with a clap of your hands.

You're now going to identify your main or overarching goal in the following exercise ...'; some people refer to this as their purpose or their superobjective. It needs to be connected at the deepest possible level to your meaning. In fact, this may be the moment where you fundamentally reappraise what gives meaning to your life. It's an old but true saying that life becomes worthwhile when you have worthwhile goals. Think about what worthwhile means to you.

In your notebook, write down your meaning and your main or overarching goal. To bring these into sharpest possible focus, you are going to employ your imagination.

Exercise 5.2: Meaning and Main Goal

Make yourself comfortable on a chair, arms on your knees or in your lap and feet flat on the floor. Take two deep breaths to centre yourself and then close your eyes.

Begin by focussing on what gives Meaning to your life. It will probably be what you identified in Chapter 1, but don't worry if it feels right for this to change.

Now imagine a world in which this meaning is everywhere – it has prevailed. Pay careful attention to what you are imagining. Over a period of three minutes, sharpen and tighten your vision of this world until it becomes more specifically related to your meaning. For example, if your meaning is tied to a philosophy or religion, is your 'world' a place where everyone shares the same morality or compassion? Exactly what does that look like? If your meaning is your family, is it a place where each and every member is happy and successful in their individual pursuits, or are they living in a close practical and emotional relationship with shared goals and interdependent achievements?

At the end of the three minutes, write down the parts of your imagining that had the deepest resonance. Which made you feel most excited? Most contented? Most comfortable? And, if highly undesirable things came into your mind, don't worry at all. Just don't focus on them. Remember, you don't have to believe and act upon everything that you think.

Have a look at what you have written. Does it feel right? If not, simply do the exercise again. Is what you have written a main goal or is it a description of your meaning? If it is the latter, spend a few minutes thinking how it can be shaped into an achievable goal or target. What can *you* do to move the world towards your vision?

For example, if your vision is something colossal or universal such as human rights prevailing or the end of world poverty, it is now deciding what you can realistically do to work towards that aim. Remember that all goals must be attainable. They can be a really tough challenge, but it must be something you can achieve. It's important that you can focus on the specific things that you can achieve rather than, in the cases above, the myriad of things that you cannot. So your main goal might be any of the following:

▶ Spreading the message of … getting as many people as you can to engage with the cause

▶ Raising as much money as you can for the cause

▶ Giving as much time/expertise as you can to the cause

If your meaning (what enables you to get up in the morning and drives you through times of adversity) is, say, the company you started four years ago, it's easier to translate this into a main goal.

Write down the main goal. Again, sit with it and change it until it feels right.

When you are happy with what's in your notebook, we'll move on to the next exercise, looking at specific goals.

Specific Goals

Many specific goals seem mundane, to do with the day-to-day of life. It may seem to you that they don't belong alongside the stuff of your dreams and your vision of the you that you want to be. For example, the goals might be:

▶ I want to get to work on time

▶ I want to stop shouting at my six-year-old

▶ I want to give up smoking

But just think of how profoundly a life can alter when small goals are achieved. The unstressful office when you have time for a tea before you begin. A calm home environment and happy six-year-old. A you that can run without getting out of breath and has enough money saved from not smoking to take a trip or two each year.

We would suggest selecting no more than three specific goals so that your energy and focus don't become dissipated. You can always add more once these are up and running. Again, if these are closely linked to the 'wants' that you wrote in Chapter 3, that's great, if not, equally fine. The main consideration is that at least some are linked as closely as possible to your main goal.

We train people in Mind Fitness in businesses, education, the performance industry and in the wider community; our teams do everything from one-off sessions to year-long projects in special schools. The number of our specific Mind Fitness goals is considerably more than three. But we always check back to the main goal and ask, 'OK, if we take on this project, is it moving us towards the goal of helping as many people as possible to get out of their own way?'

Napoleon Hill in his wonderful book *Think and Grow Rich* talks about the main goal as a boat.[1] For every goal/objective, you ask yourself, 'Is it helping the boat to go faster?'

Exercise 5.3: Specific Goals

Write down three specific goals in your notebook.

Make sure that they are Specific, Measurable, Attainable, Realistic and Time bound (SMART) Write down when they will be achieved.

They should fit well together and each should help you towards your main goal.

Reconciling goals and beliefs

It's time to think about whether your beliefs are likely to help you achieve these goals. For example, perhaps you have decided, drawing from your main goal of forwarding the issue of human rights, that you are going to write an article each week to be published in various papers, journals and the like. Do you, then, have a strong belief in your journalistic skills and persuasive abilities? If none of your five beliefs seems relevant to the goals you have chosen, this is the time to identify ones that will.

Similarly, consider if there are unhelpful beliefs not yet identified that would cause you to self-sabotage when attempting to move towards the goals. Once you have had that 'Oh I see' moment, try to frame it into a belief as you learned how to do in Chapter 4. If you have identified additional unhelpful beliefs, add these to the list.

For example, you might have set yourself the goal of running in the next marathon. But, if you are caring for an elderly parent and your belief is that family are better than carers at making your relative as happy and comfortable as possible, it is unlikely that you will make the time to train. In this case, you might try to reframe the belief to something along the lines of, 'I would prefer that my mother had family to get her ready for bed but, if twice a week it is carers, that is a compromise I am willing to accept.'

Our beliefs are often at odds with the things that we want most passionately to achieve, and it is crucial that these are identified, challenged and changed if you are going to release the huge potential you possess. Commit yourself to this process of change – the reward is the glorious picture you now have in your mind of the 'you' that can succeed at the things that are most important in your life. Once you are confident of your meaning, goals and beliefs, you have greater control of your destiny. You are a ship that knows where it's heading – the Master of your Fate, the Captain of your Soul. Your boat is moving.

Very soon you will notice that you are already feeling happier. There is a lovely saying that we absolutely endorse. Our state of wellbeing does not depend on our position in life, but on the direction in which we are heading. That means you always have to make sure that you are continuing to move towards the destiny you have chosen and the person you would like to be.

Small steps are good

It's important to make sure that not only are the goals attainable, but that you *feel* them to be so. Sometimes a big goal that will always be a long time in the coming is a hard mast on which to fix your focus and commitment. You can finish a day feeling as though you have achieved almost nothing because your efforts, however solid, have only moved you a miniscule amount along the line. Because your feeling of achievement is key to your wellbeing and, therefore, to your continued commitment, it's really important that slow progress or progress that at times seems to be slow doesn't undermine your journey.

The easiest way of avoiding this is to divide each of your goals (if needed) into smaller steps, say four to six for each target, so that the next stage always remains within reach. It's important that you hit the 'success' button with the things that really matter to you as often as you can. Achievements linked to main goals and meaning will deliver the kind of boost that sustains you on your quest, or sometimes even propels you up to the next level of commitment and belief. Take a few minutes to revisit your notebook and make the division of goals you think will work best.

The art of Course-Correct

The other real advantage of dividing your goals into smaller steps is that, if you go off target, you will soon have the opportunity to course-correct. Almost no one ever achieved anything by going in a straight unbroken line from A to B. The key then is realising that you have drifted and taking the necessary steps to move back on track as quickly as you can. And you need to do it without any self-recrimination. Instead, congratulate yourself for getting yourself back on track so soon and so skilfully. The people that are most admired in this world are masters of course-correction.

In order to course-correct, you'll have to consider what it is that has taken you off course. Self-evaluation is an important and necessary tool. Don't, however, use it as an excuse for the ANTs to invade and bog you down in past noise and negative self-talk. Keep it factual; this happened. I did this and this was the consequence. No spiralling off into blame of yourself or others, and don't open the floodgates to previous mistakes that may or may not be similar. Successful people always reflect and evaluate. They learn from their mistakes, but they do not dwell on them. Dwell on your success, not your 'failures'. In fact, start to reframe your perception of failure and success. Many phenomenally successful business men and women have 'failed' companies and business ventures behind them. These 'failures' gave them the opportunity to learn skills and techniques that make them, today, successful. If you say to yourself 'This is a new undertaking or skill – I aim to achieve the target by attempt three,' then you won't see attempt two as a failure but as a part of the process.

Recognising obstacles

As you join up your goals, beliefs and meaning you will find that you gain access to a far bigger picture. You can use this effectively to recognise obstacles and potential troubles from a much greater distance. You are sailing on a sea of infinite potential – the rocks might be extreme issues, your own negative thoughts or unhelpful beliefs. Build keeping a look-out for obstacles into your daily routine. We have to accept that there will be set-backs. If you do get blown off course, for whatever reason, just get back on track. We can easily succumb to All or Nothing Thinking – 'I've cheated on this diet and now it's all ruined. Where did I put that chocolate?' The best laid plans of mice and men can be rumbled by unforeseen circumstances, by the unpredictability of other people or even by nature herself. But in the new world order recognising them and accepting them keeps you in control. You can choose how best to respond. No more head in the sand, for that is the breeding ground of ANTs.

Not only will the picture be bigger, it will also be clearer. Use this clarity to look out for 'gaps', missing pieces of the jigsaw that you will need to complete your goal. Perhaps it is a piece of training that you need to do, a person you need to identify, a conversation that you need to have. Remember that changing a goal is OK if your obstacle is that you come to realise that it is not as powerful a motivator as you thought it would be. In fact, not revisiting goals often enough can force us, over time, to be trapped in the past, living the decisions of the person we used to be.

Changing goals is fine. Abandoning them or neglecting them is not. Too many people, as we said, have almost forgotten their hopes and dreams. These are a vital part of our wellbeing and it's hugely debilitating if we relegate them to the back of our minds like mementos in an attic.

Visualisation

The sports industry has been using goal-based visualisation techniques for more than two decades. Golfers started to practise it wholesale as far back as the 1970s.

The advent of MRI scanners means we know that, when an athlete visualises running a race, the same parts of their brain will be engaged as if they were actually running, as will the same muscle groups. As we said before, our brain does not distinguish between real and imagined experience. The implications of this are staggering.

Many sports coaches also believe that mental training programmes are, in addition, proving key to prolonging the professional career of sportsmen and women. During the inevitable periods away from training through injury, athletes can continue to train mentally, resulting in a quicker return to form and better protection of the injured muscle or bone.

NASA astronauts use visualisation as essential training, to imagine, on earth, the manoeuvres that they will be required to perform in space.[2] And many businesses are building it into their working day.

This means that imagination and creative thought can be used not only to sharpen concentration, but also as a key means to practise being the person we want to be. We can use goal-based visualisation to help us to acquire and sustain a whole array of qualities and skills.

Exercise 5.4: A Practice Visualisation

We're going to do a practice visualisation first before doing one that is directly related to your specific goals. Research shows that the clearer the picture you envisage the more effective the process. It seems to work best if you start with three key moments that you can fill with detail. You then go back and build an 'experience' by joining the three together.

We'll use something that's easy to divide into three key moments – a race. You are a 100 metre sprinter running your perfect race.

Before beginning, get yourself comfortable in the same way as before. Take two good breaths and then close your eyes.

We're going to spend a minute on each of three moments:

▶ the beginning of the race as the starting pistol goes off

▶ the middle of the race when you have just broken into the lead

▶ the end of the race where you hit the tape and win

For each of the three moments spend the minute creating all the details that you can.

▶ Moment 1. You are on the starting blocks. The gun has just gone off. What can you see, smell, hear and touch? Perhaps there is a taste in your mouth. Be specific: if the track is brown, what shade? For how long can you hear the echo of the gun? Who are the other runners?

▶ Moment 2. You are halfway through the race and have just taken the lead. How exactly is each part of your body feeling? Are the crowd cheering? Is the stadium full?

▶ Moment 3. You win the race. By how much and from which other strong competitors? Does the crowd erupt? Does exhaustion hit you or could you run it all again?

Now take these three moments and, keeping the level of detail, run it through like a film, joining the three into a race, a journey.

Exercise 5.5: Goal-Based Visualisation for Your Specific Goal

Now we'll do the exercise based on one of your specific goals. Once you've chosen which goal, think about three key moments on the way to achieving the target.

For example, one young woman we worked with always went to pieces in exams. For several months, she visualised Moment 1 – entering the exam hall and sitting down, Moment 2 – opening the paper and Moment 3 – reading the questions and knowing, beyond a shadow of a doubt, that she could answer them. She passed her finals with flying colours. By the time she got back into an exam situation, her brain expected her to be successful; it was an established neural pathway, the route of least resistance.

Identify your three moments and spend a minute on each, filling in as much detail as possible, as you did with the race.

Now extend the moments into a movie, filling in the gaps. Keep the detail. Be aware of all physical sensations and of the emotion/s you are feeling.

Your movie probably lasts a minute or two. The more often you play it through, the faster it becomes your brain's expected outcome. Try to slot it in to moments that are generally empty time, or where there is a vulnerability to fall prey to the ANTs; waiting at a bus stop, walking to the station, wherever you can make good use of the time.

Not only will it rewrite your brain to expect and accommodate success, but it is guaranteed to put you into a really good mood. Imagine how happy our athlete would be if she won a race at least once a day!

When you are vulnerable to ANTs

Not all goals have a definite end, a date when you can clap your hands together and say, 'Well that one's done and done well.' Your main goal, for example, might be to be a more compassionate person. The nature of such a goal is ongoing. If this is the case, it's even more important that you set yourself recognisable attainable markers along the way. Be sure of how you will evaluate (and reward) your success.

Conversely, be aware that, in the time immediately after a big goal is achieved, you're immensely vulnerable. For a time, perhaps a long time, you have been working towards something of value; however much you congratulate yourself, you are likely to feel it 'gone'. Many performers have their darkest moments after the last performance or a long run of a show. Many older people long for retirement only to find that they are quickly plunged into an empty world without the goals and purpose of their former life.

If you know that an important target is about to be achieved, make sure that you have another in place, and make sure you build in a daily time, for at least a month, to celebrate your achievement. Most people brush their successes under the carpet; as soon as each success is achieved, it is forgotten.

Finally, remember that it can be highly invigorating and motivating to be part of a collective goal. This can be anything from a local football team aiming for the community cup, to putting a man on the moon. But you have to be fully involved, committed by the heart, not by a contract or a begrudging promise. And it can also be a thrill to help others on the journey towards their goals. It's one of the reasons why teaching and nursing are vocations into which people throw themselves wholeheartedly, no matter how hard their day-to-day lives. To help someone achieve their potential is an astonishingly rich and rewarding experience.

Questions and Answers

▶ **Can I really be anything I want to be?**

The simple answer is no. It is really important, as we have said, that you choose goals that are attainable. Achieving them can involve every ounce of your energy and commitment, but it must be possible.

For example, we have to accept that we can't change backwards, only forwards. When we set a goal we are sometimes re-envisaging the past; it's easy to do, it's a life we know. But we have to let go, accept where we are now, where we are starting from, and move on.

It is also about prioritising. There are many things that are possible, but only if you direct a lot of your time towards the goal. We have all seen how much people can improve on TV shows like celebrity ballroom dancing or ice skating, but you have to be prepared to give several hours a day to the cause.

And, finally, it is remembering that it is about being your best self – not the best dancer in the word, but the best dancer that you can be.

> ▶ **What if duty is keeping me from achieving my goals?**
>
> People often become resentful because they feel that a sense of duty is keeping them from doing what they want to do, from achieving their goals. They have become entrenched in the view that the situation is beyond their control, beyond their changing, for example if you are the only sibling caring for an elderly parent or if you have a child with emotional difficulties or behavioural issues.
>
> We would say always pin it back to your meaning. If one of your main goals is to give your mother the best possible quality of life or your teenager the best opportunity of a stable and successful future, then hold this in your mind. Remind yourself that you have chosen this path. It won't always make the day-to-day tasks easier, but it should stop the resentment setting in. And, if you find that it does not, that the resentment persists, then perhaps it is time to reposition the main goal, to scale down what you see as achievable.
>
> If the task that is weighing you down isn't linked to your main goal or meaning, then look for ways to stop. Try to understand why it is that you see it as a duty. In the next chapter, Think your Best Think, we'll look at the myriad of things we tell ourselves to justify why changes are not possible.
>
> Learn from, but do not dwell on, missed opportunities. Remember, nothing that you have ever done is wasted. Your collective experience is what makes you the person that you are. Sometimes we have to accept that we have taken a path that wasn't the best we could have chosen, or missed another. In one short life we cannot do everything.

Conclusion

Now you're ready to set sail towards those goals. Remember always to make sure that they are attainable. We become nervous and anxious when we are trying to do the impossible. I (BW) used to write enough things on a daily to-do list to fill a week, and then beat myself up when I hadn't achieved them, even if I had got through a colossal amount. The Mind Fitness programme will 'give' you a substantial amount of extra time because you will no longer be spending huge parts of your life battling with the ANTs and following your brain down rabbit holes. It is still, however, vital to make sure that you are realistic in your expectations. You want to give yourself every chance, and to celebrate each and every success on the way – these will power you forward and just as importantly make sure that you enjoy the journey.

6

Think your best think

How to reframe your thoughts to make the most of situations and opportunities

You have learned how Neuroplasticity will allow you to change, really change. You have identified the negative unhelpful beliefs that you have been dragging around for goodness knows how long and you know how, using the ABC Model, to challenge and change them. You have thought about what happens from here, what path you want to take; you have set new goals that will take you to this 'new' you and you have imagined yourself as the calm, confident, successful and happy person that you can be.

This chapter is about making sure that your path towards this goal is as smooth as it can possibly be; to make sure that your old self is not hiding in the shadows waiting to trip you up! The whole Mind Fitness programme is, in many ways and on many levels, about learning to get out of your own way. It is particularly true in terms of reframing old patterns of thinking and repositioning unconscious bias.

Unless you are already familiar with the ways that Cognitive Distortions or Thinking Errors work, or unless you have recently arrived from a planet further along the neural path than we are, I think this chapter will surprise you. Most of us genuinely believe that we know the way our minds work and are aware of the prejudices and biases that influence our thoughts and feelings. You might find this is not the case! But it is surprisingly easy to clear the path. Not that any of us will get to the point where we have no bias or are completely devoid of unhelpful ways of thinking – not unless we've come from that far away planet.

What are Thinking Errors?

Thinking Errors[1] or Cognitive Distortions (both CBT terminology) are strong habitual patterns of thought that will feel to you right and normal, but are, in fact, based on false logic. Say that sentence to yourself slowly.

They are incredibly important because they can determine how we see ourselves and how we view the world. They can cause us to fail even if we have set positive goals that we are working towards, and it is likely that we will be totally unaware of them. Often Thinking Errors have caused us to 'tell' ourselves that we are not good enough, which means that self-criticism has become our main strategy to succeed; a strategy that we know now is likely to have caused unnecessary distress. But it can be changed.

In this chapter, we are going to go through the most common Thinking Errors. There is a short set exercise that you can use at the end of each 'error' to reframe your thinking if this is required. We'll also look at two mindsets that come up a lot in our training sessions, procrastination and perfectionism, and explore ways to turn these around if either of these are stopping you from realising your potential.

First, we'll think about how we came to have illogical biases in our thinking and how we can become aware of what they are.

As we've said before, our brain builds our vision of the world from past thoughts and experiences. Although the brain gathers input from both positive and negative situations, because of the way the ANTs set in negative biases are much more common. Because our emotions are often more highly charged in a negative situation, these biases, essentially negative slants on the world that would not be borne out by evidence, become stronger in times of crisis and become major symptoms in acute anxiety and depression.

Cognitive Distortions or Thinking Errors are often the beginning of an automatic loop. Thoughts lead to feelings, which lead to physiological symptoms, which lead to behaviours, which lead to thoughts, and so we go round again.

For example:

Thought
'Nobody likes me in my new workplace.'

Feeling
'I feel self-conscious all the time.'

Physiological symptom
'I'm sweating and blushing far more than usual.'

Behaviour
'I'm staying away from them as much as I can.'

Thought
'There's something wrong with me. People didn't like me at my old office either.'

Feeling
'I feel very anxious and unhappy.'

Physiology
'My heart is beating fast and I feel dizzy.'

Behaviour
'I eat my lunch at my desk avoiding social contact with colleagues.'

Thought
'I might stay off work tomorrow.'

It happens because the information that exists about any topic is colossal and, in this digital culture, is growing almost exponentially. Our brain is programmed to select for us the information that it believes we require. There is no other way that we could survive. But, of course, it chooses selectively, based on the information and connecting emotional responses already stored. The automatic process works in patterns, based on the cumulative effect of everything you have been exposed to throughout your life. In other words, our brains take helpful short cuts and in doing so trip us up.

The vast majority of bias is unconscious. Think about this for a moment. We can be biased about a myriad of issues and not even know it. In fact, the most dangerous thing about bias is exactly this – our lack of awareness. Almost all of us believe we can outsmart it. I know I did. For example, just think of the number of people you know who say, 'I don't see race.' This simply won't be true if you are over five.

The 'I Just Know' State of Mind

At the core of the problem is the belief that you *know something*. Believing that you know something, in fact whole hosts of things, is fundamental to the way you navigate the world. We simply don't look to see if there is evidence that could point us in another direction and, if we saw such a thing, we would probably assume that it was wrong.

Many scientists believe that this is considerably more of a problem in the information age. While science works as an evidence pyramid, going through several robust stages to examine, prove and test that something is a fact, we are increasingly relying on the internet and social media. In many cases it is one person's opinion, but we have started to believe that the plural of anecdote is data.

Our intrinsic bias depends on our culture, religion, environment and, as we have said, on every experience that we have ever had. In terms of the huge amounts of information that is out there, we selectively consume that which supports our opinion and selectively ignore that which attacks it. And this happens in the automatic part of our brain.

It leads us to the incredibly powerful belief – 'I just know' – with masses of emotion invested in it. And of course we try to pass this on because we are convinced that it is right. Even newspapers, which have their own bias because they are written by humans, are fulfilling this drive – 'I just know this and I want you to just know it too.'

If we are really going to stop getting in our own way we must be willing to recognise our own biases and try to see past them.

As we have said earlier, behind all the biases is a mental shortcut. The Availability Heuristic Bias is relying on information that comes to mind quickly. If there is a number of related events or situations that spring into your thoughts when you are making a decision, you give greater credence to this information. If something is in the news or has been repeated many times on social media, it will spring to mind. It is why, for example, most people would think being a police officer is a far more dangerous job than being a logger, while the reverse is in fact true. Equally surprising, due to our availability bias, is finding out that more people are killed by cows each year than by terrorists.

The Bandwagon Bias is a kind of groupthink, based on the rule that behaviours and beliefs spread among people just as trends do. As more people come to believe something others jump on the bandwagon, despite the lack of underlying evidence or sometimes even in the face of a strong counter argument. We don't analyse the information. We just step on board. One of the strongest examples of the Bandwagon Effect is in politics, where a campaign that is on the 'up' can gather speed and supporters incredibly fast.

How we can change Distorted Thinking

As we have seen, irrational thoughts lead to problematic emotional states and, when we are stressed, our thinking becomes dramatic and extreme. It doesn't match up with the reality of what is going on around us. This in itself is distressing and disconcerting which, of course, leads to more stress and more irrational thoughts. Anger management is heavily dependent on reframing distorted thinking. When you are next stressed, take a moment to notice your thoughts and try to search out any distorted thinking.

So how can we make a real and lasting change to the distorted thinking that our brains throw up, often at the most inconvenient times?

The first step is simply awareness, an understanding that, although what you are thinking feels absolutely right, it may not be logical, helpful or even true. The fact that you are reading this book means that you are already on the path.

The second step is labelling, which is why we're going to list all the common Thinking Errors. If we can really pin them down we start to be aware of them even as they come into our mind; we can deal with them specifically, relating them to any unhelpful beliefs we may be holding.

The third step is monitoring; make a note in your notebook of when they came and how often. It is likely that you will start to see patterns and triggers. Make sure you know in what situations your three most frequent Thinking Errors usually occur.

Once you are at this level of awareness they can be reframed.

The Thinking Errors exercise detailed at the end of the Thinking Errors section can be undertaken for any one of them, as needed. You can work your way through – reading the information then doing the exercise. This will give you a full understanding of what these distortions are and how they fit together. Or you can read all of the list but just focus on doing the exercise for the two or three that you think most apply to you.

The most common Thinking Errors[2]

As you will see, there are a number of links and overlaps between the Thinking Errors listed below. Some practitioners group these together, while others work them separately. If you know that you habitually use one Thinking Error, it is worth testing yourself on those that seem to you to be linked.

All or Nothing Thinking

If you fall prey to All or Nothing Thinking, there is no middle ground. You are likely to frequently use words such as 'always, never, forever'. Pay particular attention if the thinking is linked to the perception of self-worth – 'I'm a complete failure.'

An example would be believing that you are a terrible employee because you took a day off work. This is linked to Polarising or Black and White Thinking. You will see everything in terms of success or failure; moral issues are black and white. Shades of grey do not exist. All or Nothing Thinking is also linked to Perfectionism, which we will look at later.

Overgeneralisation

People who fall prey to overgeneralisation will take an isolated case or single event, take it as evidence and use it to form a universal conclusion.

Common examples of overgeneralisation are:

'All men/women are the same.'

'We're always fighting.'

Taking one unsuccessful job interview or relationship to mean that 'I'm never going to get a job' or believing I'm never going to find a partner'.

Mental Filter

The Mental Filter is when we magnify the negatives and filter out the positives of any situation. This is sometimes called the Magnification Bias or the Binocular Trick. This leads to the glass half-empty mindset and it is very easy to fall into. For example, if we give a presentation (a performance or any activity in a public arena) and 95 per cent of the audience liked what we did but 5 per cent didn't, we will dwell, if we allow ourselves to, on the criticism of the few who did not. It is one of the things that most powerfully convinces us that we are never doing well enough.

Jumping to Conclusions

Jumping to Conclusions is thinking that you know the outcome (really know it) from little or no data evidence. It is often assuming the worst and commonly has its most powerful negative effects when it is linked to the way we think people feel about us. Often it can show us that our Self-Image is not as robust as it could be. We'll look at this in Chapter 7 Feel Positive. For example, a partner arriving home late can lead us to the conclusion that he or she is having an affair. A room becoming quiet (or seeming to do so) as we walk in can convince us that everyone was talking about us. This can also be linked to Personalisation.

Jumping to Conclusions is comprised mostly of Mind Reading: He didn't say good morning today so he must be mad at me', and Fortune Telling: 'It's inevitable that I'll fail my driving test again'.

Often the feeling will serve up evidence that simply isn't true. For example, taking the driving test line above, it may lead to, 'I'm bound to fail my driving test again as my driving has got worse since the last time I took it.'

We feel convinced that our predictions are an already established fact. In these situations it's always worth making a note of what you actually know. This may take a couple of attempts at stripping back to remove all conjecture. If you had to speak impartially about it at a 'trial', what could you actually say?

Sometimes Discounting the Positive is looked at as a separate Thinking Error. If you know you do one more than the other, either magnify the negatives or discount the positives, then concentrate on that.

Sometimes this can be determined by a belief that we don't deserve the positive and so we literally cannot believe it. If someone is nice to us, for example, we will assume that they have a hidden agenda.

Should Be Statements

Should Be Statements are linked to the rigid demands that we looked at when we were learning the ABC Model.

In most cases, they are linked to a belief that others 'should' believe our personal rules, which, as we have seen, we have no control over. We feel that people 'should' be grateful, 'must' say thank you and 'ought' to behave appropriately.

These may be personal rules that have been handed down to us and don't fit in with the person we are now, leading to a huge amount of pressure and guilt – 'I must get into university', 'I should be a better daughter', 'I have to cope better with a family and a demanding job'.

It can also be a way that we motivate ourselves: 'I must finish this essay by 8 pm' or in the case of bad managers, 'a competent clerk ought to be able to work more efficiently'.

If you are using your 'shoulds' as a stick to beat yourself with, as we often do, it's worth asking yourself if you would place the same demands on a loved one in a similar situation.

Labelling/Mislabelling

Labelling or Mislabelling is an extreme form of All or Nothing Thinking or Overgeneralisation. Labelling involves language that is highly coloured and emotionally loaded, which often leads to a step-up in the negative emotion. An example would be saying 'I'm a loser' rather than 'I made a mistake' or 'he's a loser' rather than 'he could have behaved more pleasantly or appropriately'.

From the moment that we have defined ourselves or another person as the label, we are increasingly convinced of the justification. For example, the more times we refer to a work colleague with whom we disagree as a total idiot, the more deeply we will believe it.

Emotional Reasoning

Emotional Reasoning is one of the most powerful Thinking Errors. Almost all of us believe that if we feel something strongly it must be true. Instinctively, a powerful emotional response 'proves' to us that we are right to hold that opinion, and this is even more likely to be the case if what we are feeling is an Unhealthy Negative Emotion. We'll have a look at these in Chapter 11. 'I feel it' translates all too naturally to 'I know it'. The fact that we feel so jealous 'convinces' us that the affair we have suspected is true. It is therefore one of the hardest Thinking Errors to recognise in ourselves. In fact, sometimes it is easier to move the other way, from the negative emotion to the thought, to ask yourself next time you are angry, 'Is there anything that my anger makes me absolutely convinced of?' Emotional Reasoning can also lead to self-fulfilling prophecy, 'I feel stupid so I must be stupid', leading us to behave stupidly.

Personalisation

Personalisation is where we see ourselves as the cause of external events, often unhealthy events. It often results in us blaming ourselves for things that are out of our control and for this reason it is sometimes called the Mother of Guilt. It can lead to an enormous amount of regret, lots of 'if only I hadn't' when, in fact, our actions have had little or no effect on the situation. Other emotions and feelings that spring from Personalisation are shame and inadequacy. Personalisation is also often associated with narcissistic traits as people who fall prey to this Thinking Error can see themselves at the centre of the universe. There may also be a strong tendency to worry about what other people think.

Certainly a chief cause of unhappiness is taking things personally that were not meant personally at all. For, example, a piece of constructive criticism from a manager can seem like a personal attack. Those who Personalise may see themselves as long-suffering victims. Personalisation is often linked to blaming, either yourself or other people. Try to be aware for a week or so of where you place the responsibility for the events that occur in your life. To break this cycle, never allow yourself to attribute more than 25 per cent of the 'blame' or 'causation' to any one person or event.

Low Frustration Tolerance

This springs from a belief that things must be the way we want them to be or life will be intolerable. How often do we say to ourselves, 'I can't stand it' or 'I can't bear it when. . . .'? It's a huge factor in the creation of both stress and anger.

Low Frustration Tolerance is often found in relation to minor situations and inconveniences, rather than crises. Because minor inconveniences happen all the time, it can lead to a state of almost constant irritation, which builds to an occasional explosion. Again, it is about changing our perspective. Think how glad we would be to stand in a queue if we were receiving provisions in a disaster zone. If you know that you have Low Frustration Tolerance, then notice your thoughts, the patterns and the language, and work, using the exercise, to change the 'script'.

Awfulising

Awfulising is linked to Mental Filter, Magnification/Minimalisation. Some people call it Catastrophising. It is probably the most common Thinking Error and it's well worth tackling. We almost all have a tendency to feel that situations and events are much worse than they really are. If we can get this in check, then the cup really does become much more than half full.

Addressing Awfulising is essentially about asking ourselves the question 'How awful is it really?' In training sessions, we use the example of a large-scale redundancy that Andy helped people with. If 100 people are made redundant, they will, of course, all have different responses. If they have to put the redundancy on a scale of 1–10, where 1 is that it's not awful at all and 10 is that it is the worst it can be, the reactions would span the scale. It would range from those who were glad to take the redundancy package through to some who were terrified that they would not be able to feed their family. Let's take a relatively minor event, cracking the screen of your phone. Something like this can seem 'awful' whereas really it's expensive and annoying but nobody dies.

Our teams do a lot of work in schools with students just before their GCSEs and A levels. If you ask them how they rate their forthcoming exams, most will say 'really awful', a 9 or a 10. If they are then asked to imagine that they are living in a war zone where their family is under constant threat, where they might not have a roof over their head or enough to eat, and ask them to score this, most say 10. We then ask them to rescore their exams. Most change the number to a 2 or 3. It's about altering our perception.

Exercise 6.1: Awfulising

Before we start, let's take an example. Let's say the football team you support has been relegated. Give a number 1 response – this could be, 'Well, I suppose it was bound to happen. They have been 10 years in the Premier League.' Now give a number 10 response – for example, 'No! I can't believe this; it's all the fault of the manager, he should be shot!' It's actually quite fun and you get an amazing sense of control by adjusting your reactions.

Write yourself a set of 10 cards, each with an issue or situation. Perhaps two or three of these can be directly related to your current circumstances. Now write a set of cards with the numbers 1–10 and shuffle them. Place these in two piles.

First, turn over a situation and then a number. Try to give an appropriate response.

It's a great exercise for helping us to realise that many of the problems we have in our life are not as bad as we immediately think. It helps us to see patterns and identify where our tendencies lie. It helps us to be aware that we choose, every hour of every day, how we will react to any situation.

Start to build this into your daily life. When the coffee machine is out of order or you get caught at a red light, just give yourself that moment to ask 'how awful is it really?'

Exercise 6.2: Thinking Errors

This exercise can be done for any/all of the Thinking Errors.

1 Write a statement that gives a clear example of whichever Thinking Error you are working on. If you can't think of one, it's fine to use one of the examples given in the paragraph describing the Thinking Error, but it's useful if you have one that relates to you and your situation. For example – 'Without my phone contacts no one will be able to contact me and I'll go mad.'

   Statement: _____

2 Replace the statement with one that deals with the same topic but that covers the middle ground – in other words, which states the same 'fact', 'belief' or 'opinion' in a less extreme way.

   Statement: _____

3 Replace this statement with one that runs counter to this 'fact', 'belief' or 'opinion' – in other words which states the opposite.

   Statement: _____

4 Imagine what a third party would say or do about this opinion. Pick a person. What would they say or do?

   Statement: _____

5 If this statement is one that you hold to or have held to in the past, identify the belief that underpins it.

   Belief: _____

   Make a note of whether this belief is current or has been challenged/changed.

   Note: _____

   Creative Response 1

6 Write a six-line script that shows a negative consequence of practising this Thinking Error. Limit yourself to two characters, each saying three short sentences.

   (If you hold to this statement, it's useful to make one of the characters in the script you.)

   Creative Response 2

7 Write a six-line script that shows the positive consequence of practising the way of thinking that runs counter to this statement.

Again, limit yourself to two characters, each saying three short sentences.

We're going to finish the chapter by having a quick look at two ways of thinking that can have a severe impact on our lives – Procrastination and Perfectionism.

Procrastination

Procrastination is the act of putting off doing something that you know should be done now. This is different from planned delay when there may be a perfectly good reason to wait until a certain task can happen. For this reason, procrastination has been referred to as the thief of time.

Procrastination can range from mildly annoying selective time wasting (I'll just have another coffee before I get on with it) to being a serious issue that can lead to personal unhappiness, lost opportunities and chronic life-inhibiting inertia.

The assumption is that the inability to get a task done in good time can be blamed on laziness. But it's often about busying ourselves with tasks that we prefer doing while avoiding the most pressing chores that we don't relish. 'I was so busy, I didn't have time to get the job done!' It could be classed as selective prioritisation.

The reasons why we procrastinate can be complex and varied, but understanding more about the causes of this troublesome inhibitor to productive self-management will allow us to begin making changes. Perfectionism can be a cause. It's never going to be good enough so we delay starting. Along with that, the need for comfort – Low Frustration Tolerance. Having to be in the right mood, to feel motivated. I'll do it tomorrow when I'm bound to be more up for it. Having the knowledge, immediate understanding or perceived capability to start a task. Many of us need instant gratification. If we're not enjoying the task, we stop, defer to another time. These are Cognitive Distortions and therefore Mind Fitness exercises, especially the ABC Model, are highly effective in increasing our ability to get out of our own way and get moving.

Exercise 6.3: For Procrastinators

List three tasks that you have been putting off.

Imagine the future you that accomplishes the tasks.

Procrastinators often feel, when imagining a future self, that this person is somehow a stranger. This is because they know that they will not be that person without investing in change.

As you imagine your future self, build in a few recognisable traits; keep doing the exercise until this future self feels comfortable. Remember, the future you is always you. You are just releasing the potential.

Perfectionism

As we've seen, perfectionists are often also chronic procrastinators as they put off undertaking tasks until the conditions are perfect, which, of course, they never are. Perfection can never be achieved.

Many perfectionists also wear it as a badge of honour. 'Oh, but I'm a perfectionist,' they'll tell us at training sessions. Perfectionism is, in fact, a dangerous ideal and it's a punishing way to live, and extremely hard to be around. Most perfectionists feel themselves to be chronically failing most of the time.

When we are young and looking about for our role models, and when we are learning anything new, we follow a picture of those that have done it best – the masters. We do this in both our personal and professional lives. But we are seeing these people at the height of their success; it is a narrative of achievement. We do not see their early drafts, failures, fears and despair and so we under budget the difficulty of achieving anything close to their standards. While aiming high is good, it is essential that we look properly at the difficulty of anything we choose to undertake and allow ourselves time to get there. If we don't, we will torture ourselves for failures that are inevitable. We have to allow ourselves to be mediocre or even inadequate on the way to success and, as we have said before, we have to recognise the necessary and legitimate role of failure in our process of learning. We must trust ourselves to keep inspired and course-correct. As you undertake a task at home or at work, give it a difficulty score. Then, afterwards, you can say,' It was difficult, but I knew it would be.' We torture ourselves only if we thought it would be easier.

And, of course, although many tasks, projects and undertakings of new learning are incredibly difficult and complex, they will be achieved more easily when you have changed distorted thinking to rational thinking and stopped getting in your own way.

Exercise 6.4: Thinking Errors Statements

Give a typical statement from someone who suffers from:

1 I Just Know State of Mind

2 Should Be Statements

3 All or Nothing Thinking

4 Personalisation

5 Low Frustration Tolerance

6 Awfulising

7 Procrastination

8 Perfectionism

Questions and Answers

▶ **Is there a danger of going from being a procrastinator (or regularly procrastinating) to so super-efficient and effective that I become manically over driven?**

Mind Fitness is all about rationality. So, the answer is no, not if you don't want to be like that. I (AB) once worked with a well-known actor and author who was super productive. He planned his days meticulously, writing efficiently by day and arriving breezily at the theatre for the evening performance where he spent time off stage researching and reading. He was an incredible chap, wonderfully talented and amazingly driven. I'd say that he'd be classed as a workaholic and I'm also sure that his phenomenal output and workload gave his life huge meaning. He made those choices in his lifestyle and always appeared to be an extremely happy, balanced and fulfilled man. That approach worked well for him. But workaholism can be dangerous if it leads to anxiety and stress. Balance is the key. Will you stop procrastinating entirely? Probably not. Can you reduce the instances of procrastination in your life? Most certainly. It's striking the balance that's important. Being happy is the ultimate goal.

▶ **But surely if I give up being a perfectionist then I'm settling for second best?**

Leading yourself away from the destructive path of perfection in no way means that you are settling for second best. It is something that people are often worried about, particularly in a professional capacity where they are expected to have the very highest standards.

We know that goals must be achievable; perfectionism is not. It can be the hardest challenge, the biggest reach, but it must be possible. You can strive for excellence and, just once in a while, you can touch its coat-tail. But demand perfectionism of yourself or others and you are condemning both you and them to failure and a huge amount of stress along the way. It is also likely that, rather than keep you motivated, the demand for perfection will do the opposite; as you realise it is unachievable, your levels of interest and engagement will begin to wane.

Chapter Recap

Spend a few minutes thinking through these questions:

1 To which of the distortions are you most vulnerable?

2 How does it/do they affect your life?

3 Why do you think it's harmful?

4 Do you generally have a more distorted view of yourself or others?

5 Why do you think this is?

Conclusion

If you catch your thoughts taking you towards the old *you*, just buy yourself a minute of reflection time by doing one of the mindfulness exercises – Image Breathing, NOW or Foxhole in My Mind.

The turning point comes when a distorted thought can be noticed and examined, but it has produced no emotional or physiological response. Sometimes, uncovering a distortion or bias now makes me laugh. 'I'm thinking what? Good grief!' It's like being able to see into the mind of a mischievous, but not malevolent, child. So reposition, reframe, course-correct and off you go. And the best thing is the confidence from knowing that, whatever comes along (and it will), you can look after yourself by thinking your best think.

Feel positive

How to be positive on the deepest possible level and use that positivity to release your best self

Positivity and Optimism

In many ways, the whole book is about positivity – it is about you claiming tools that you can use in order to engage positively with the world. We'd love you to get up in the morning with a sense of joy. Every morning. Or as many mornings as is possible in our flawed human world. But it isn't about looking on the bright side, and it certainly isn't about pretending that the bad stuff doesn't exist or sweeping it under the carpet. Positive psychology is a powerful and pragmatic strategy that changes the way you think and the way that you respond to the things that happen in your life.

More and more healthcare professionals are seeing good mental health as a set of skills that we can acquire by learning to look after ourselves. We all give our children an enormous amount of gifts, skills, information and help because what we want most is for them to be happy, to have a good life. But we don't think to give them a mindset and a bunch of tools to make this possible – to enable them to have a positive outlook and to cope if the times get tough.

There are still some sceptics who look on positivity as a superficial garment that can be worn but wouldn't survive the first storm. Not so.

Rational thinking recognises both positive and negative thought and emotion. Positivity can be rational in that realistic thinking can be infused with a sense of optimism; optimism that comes from all that you do being fastened down to your values and the meaning you have chosen for your life. Nothing could be deeper. The fact that this thinking is rational and realistic is important; when things are bleak, our instinct can be to pull away from the positive. In these situations, hold on to your vision of the rational, as this can drive positive change.

We think that the most important thing that keeps you positive is the confidence in your own abilities. Understanding this is why, essentially, this book works. There are two mindsets based on hope when a crisis or even an everyday trouble comes along. One is the blind assumption that 'it will get better' or that 'something or someone will come along to save the day'. A good many of us have had this belief since we were children, when the something that would come along was mum or dad. The other, as we know, is the confidence to know that you will be able to pull yourself back up. You know how to do it and you know you have enough resilience to course-correct, to learn and to go forwards. Knowing this makes it so much easier to weather any storm. (And we will recognise a real storm and won't attribute the word to a simple shower.)

As we know from the previous chapters, the way we look at the world is a choice. We choose to have a good day, a good week, a good month. And in this very short life, why wouldn't we? When we are positive, we are fluid, moving, not trapped in an event; part of the solution rather than the problem. There's an insightful quote from Abraham Lincoln. 'We can complain because rose bushes have thorns, or rejoice because thorn bushes have roses.'

To feel positive you need to change your unhelpful beliefs and of course it's far easier to change your beliefs when you are feeling positive. If you find that you are not, stop for a moment and do a quick mindfulness exercise to bring you back into the appreciation of now.

Researchers have also found that positivity is the key to perseverance. It gives you the power to bust past the obstacles and to just keep on going, seeing options and opportunities along the way. Optimistic people always seem to have more energy, more charisma. Some companies even hire for optimism and positivity, making this a main focus of the personality tests that are becoming a mainstay of the hiring process.

Without positivity, all that you do will always feel like a slog, an uphill battle; and, even if you finally nail the achievement, it will come with a sense of relief rather than joy. 'Thank God now I can collapse' rather than 'Yay!'

And, of course, optimism is incredibly courageous (as is the opposite, so bat it away!) Your optimism can have a massive effect on other people, infusing them with motivation and a feeling of security as well as happiness. Positive teachers are the best in the world. I bet you can remember one or two.

> ### Exercise 7.1: Positive Jar
>
> This is an exercise that you can do at home with your family. Find a container and designate it the 'Positive Jar'. At the end of the day, each member of the family or household writes something good that happened that day and puts it in the jar. At the end of the week, take time to sit down together for 10 minutes and read them out. I have never done this without laughing. We promise that, as well as feeling good, you'll learn something about the people that you live with.

Linking Positivity to Beliefs and Thinking Errors

It is easy to see how positivity is closely linked to reframing our thoughts. How we see a problem will depend on three things:

▶ Permanence – How permanent is the problem?

▶ Pervasiveness – How pervasive is it? How much will it affect everything else in your life?

▶ Personalisation – Is it your fault?

As we have seen with the ABC and the Awfulising Exercise in Chapter 6, it's not the event but the way we respond, the way we explain it to ourselves, that counts. If, for example, the car has broken down and our thinking is positive, we will know that it isn't permanent, it will have only a very limited effect on other areas of our life and it wasn't our fault. Cars break down. The first one is most important. An issue certainly needs attention if you're seeing it as permanent. When we think the problem is permanent, we don't see any point in taking action to change it. With pervasiveness, it's often a question of Negative Self-Talk. The ANTs are apt to make a local phenomenon spread to the rest of your life!

And, of course, pessimists practise Selective Thinking – they constantly discount the positive. I would say, in fact, that most of us fall into this trap, at least in the West. We learn from an early age to be modest and even humble. We think we need this quality in order to be liked. This is one of the reasons that so many of our successes and achievements almost pass us by. We don't want to be boastful and so we don't call them out, even to ourselves. We should sing them from the rooftops, even if it is only in our hearts.

Positivity is, of course, also linked to the types of unconscious cognitive bias described in Chapter 6. So many of us, for example, feel uncomfortable in a gathering of strangers. This links back to the fear and distrust of strangers that is instilled in most of us as children. It's time to discard such limiting, outdated conditioning. Encounter these strangers with an open mind. Listen to what they say. Have a ball!

Accept, Acknowledge, Appreciate

Positivity is both the root and aim of mindfulness. The three tenets of mindfulness are Accept, Acknowledge and Appreciate.

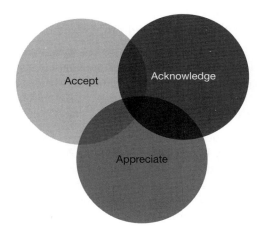

Acceptance is the basis of any programme of transformation. Unless we accept our current situation, we can't know what the proper actions are to take us to a better place. Acceptance sounds very easy but is, in fact, incredibly hard. We are talking about active recognition not passive resignation. I'd like you to think about something negative that has happened in your life, something that you genuinely believe you have accepted. If thinking about it makes you feel uncomfortable, if you start to feel tense, then you probably haven't.

The tension caused by not accepting can have serious consequences. In extreme cases, it leads to psychosis and PTSD. If you aren't working from a point of acceptance, it will always feel as though you are trying to push a square peg into a round hole.

This is why it's important to sit with a negative emotion, just that, to sit with it. Allow yourself to feel the emotion for say 20 or 30 minutes. But don't allow your thoughts to take you from that sadness or pain into a negative spiral of self-talk. Keep the ANTs at bay. In fact, sometimes it is the pain itself that gets missed out in the scrabble to recovery. We get so lost in the role of self-critic that we don't allow ourselves to properly feel. From vague recognition we move straight into problem-solving mode or else we deflect the problem altogether and move on to something else. Even with physical pain, scientists believe that acceptance is the gateway to change for patients suffering from long-term chronic pain.[1]

Acceptance is also a fundamental part of the ABC Model that we have learned, the process of changing and challenging our beliefs. When we change a rigid demand, 'my boss must not shout at me', to a preference, 'I would prefer that my boss didn't shout at me', we are accepting that we can't control the behaviour of others. Once this acceptance becomes real, grounded, options always start to appear.

We find it useful to use Positive Affirmation, which we will look at later in this chapter, to speed up the process of acceptance. Stating out loud, for example, 'I accept that I cannot change Jane's tendency to fly off the hook when she is stressed' can really help us to stay calm and in control the next time it is put to the test.

When we consciously acknowledge something we validate it. We are saying, 'It's OK that I felt really hurt when that happened.' It's especially important when we are working to accept things about ourselves: 'It's OK that I made a rash decision when I left my partner.' We have to acknowledge it all, good and bad, own it and then move on. We will look at appreciation in the section on gratitude. At this point, suffice to say, it's the stuff of religions and unconditional love. If there is magic in this world, it is gratitude.

Self-Image and Self-Worth

We are literally hypnotised, programmed by our Self-Image, by the way we see ourselves. It determines the way we behave and the way we feel. There is no boulder more likely to be getting in your way than a negative Self-Image. And, even if you think your Self-Image is pretty robust, there are likely to be a number of dents and scrapes that you are not even aware of. But it can be changed, and there is no better way than through the fusion of CBT and mindfulness.

A strong Self-Image is linked to the identification of positive beliefs and the acceptance that we have already talked about. It is linked to the bringing together of goals, meaning and beliefs. It is vital that the *you* you choose to be, the life you choose to live, is authentic. Sincerity is based on self-honesty and self-understanding. Once you find this authenticity, once you unlock you, there is an ease and grace to life that enriches all that you do and enables you to achieve your true potential.

Exercise 7.2: How Do You See Yourself?

In your notebook, draw a little picture of yourself or paste in a photograph if you prefer.

Now choose 10 things about yourself, trivial or important, although I would say that everything about you is important. For example, you might write:

▶ I paint inspiriting pictures.

▶ I am a good mother.

▶ I am getting better at holding my temper and becoming more patient.

Write these down, coming out from the you on the page.

Afterwards, read them through and give a tick to the ones that feel absolutely right, authentic. For the ones that don't, make changes until they really sit with an honest perception of yourself.

It is likely that the 10 things are not the same as the ones you would have written before beginning Chapter 1. Through identifying and changing our beliefs, through practising the gentle mindfulness meditation and through engaging your imagination in the visualisation of the you that you are becoming, your Self-Image will already have begun to change. And it will continue to do so through the rest of the book and the six-week follow-up programme and probably through the rest of your life. Once you're into the habit of identifying the negative beliefs that determine the way you see yourself, you will start to deal with them automatically as they come up and your Self-Image will continue to get stronger.

Our Self-Image is often inaccurate because our minds are full, as we have seen, of false information. A negative Self-Image may also come from the feeling, mentioned before, that we shouldn't boast, shouldn't stand out. If we hide our light under a bushel, it won't take long before we forget it is there. We must accept, really accept, that holding a low opinion of ourselves isn't a virtue but a vice.

Self-Worth

How we build and frame our Self-Image depends, to a large extent, on the way we value ourselves – our actions and, beyond this, our essential 'nature'. It depends on how the critic within us functions and whether we allow it to play a positive or negative role in our lives.

This following exercise was devised by Arnold Lazarus. It is called 'Big I Little I'.[2] The person being coached begins by drawing a large capital I with plenty of space to write inside it. This, the Big I, is the way we define

ourselves, the over-arching statement, the way we think of ourselves deep down. For so many people, what they write outside the Big I is a self-damning statement.

Let's say, in this case, that the Big I is, 'I am a monster because I walked out on my first wife after cheating on her.' The next stage is to fill the Big I with lots of Little I's. Each of those represents something positive about the person, big or small. These might be:

- ▶ I am a good husband to my second wife.
- ▶ I play a positive role in the lives of my children who I love to bits.
- ▶ I work hard at my job.
- ▶ I support two or three charities that I give a small amount to each month.
- ▶ I look out for my friends and help them whenever I can.
- ▶ I believe in looking after the environment and do my bit to recycle and spread the message.
- ▶ I love to learn and approach new subjects with curiosity.

The way we value ourselves tends to work around the Big I. For so many of us the way we define ourselves is based on one thing. This can be big or small, deep or shallow. We all know people who define themselves by the amount of money they have or the cars that sit on their driveway.

Self-Worth is about finding the evidence, the Little I's, to support you as an individual. There will always be redeeming features in your life, your actions and your beliefs. It is important to bring these forward, test them, make sure they are real and current, and then use them as a valuable ingredient of your all-important Self-Worth. Yes, there will be negative things that you have done. They don't, and must not, define you. You are a fallible human being. In the section on self-compassion, we will look at the importance of 'forgiving' yourself. The essential first step is to understand that one action or facet of your personality is not you. The key is unconditional self-acceptance.

Exercise 7.3: Big I, Little I

It's time for you to do the Big I, Little I exercise. Start with the Big I and write at the side of it a big overarching defining statement, something negative that you believe to be true. It's important to be as honest as you possibly can with yourself. If there is something that lurks at the back of your mind, perhaps even something that you have learned through iron self-discipline to banish from your brain whenever the picture of it starts to form, bring it out now. The feeling in your stomach will pass.

Now start to fill the Big I with the Little I's – as many as you can. It doesn't matter if they seem small or insignificant; these are the things that make a rounded and worthwhile human being. You have a rescue dog, buy organic, occasionally take a neighbour to the shops. Yesterday you held your nerve when you served a customer who, if not rude, was certainly unpleasant. For those of you who have children or perhaps parents that you care for, you could probably fill up a book.

Read again through the Little I's – they are you. It is time to step away from the overarching statement and value yourself more accurately. You have the evidence on the page. There are a myriad of things that are part of you, some more positive than others. You are human. And, now, by recognising your self-worth and strengthening your Self-Image, you can make sure that the *you* that moves into the future is the you that inspires you, the you that is sincere and committed to change and brimming with potential.

At Mind Fitness courses, we think about Self-Image and self-worth rather than self-esteem. As a society, we have been inclined to give a negative connotation to the notion of self-esteem. It is the way we estimate ourselves in comparison with our estimation of others. It is a relative valuation. Self-Worth does not need to be comparative in any sense. There are plenty of good deeds, good qualities and good aspirations to go around! Thinking that I am a good trainer does not have to mean that I think that I'm better than anyone else. There are lots of inspirational teachers and mentors; I've had the very good fortune of working with quite a few.

This tendency towards comparison and the resulting self-deprecation has been intensified by social media beyond anything we could have imagined. A growing army of people find themselves miserably failing in contrast to the wonderful people with their wonderful lives who parade themselves before them each day on their phones – and falling, if not sinking, into an addiction to 'likes' and peer approval.

Some people, when they're building the new more positive Self-Image, find it useful to step away for a time from social media. If you cannot do this, find a way to protect yourself from damage to the way you see and value yourself. For example, find an inspirational quote to post or information on inspirational people that you can share. Make it a challenge to yourself to give at least twice as many likes as you receive, but remember to keep them real.

It isn't about silencing the critic within you. As we have said in previous chapters, that critic is essential to the acceptance of where you are and to your ability to note when you have gone off track and quickly course-correct. But it is keeping the critic from attacking you. In Chapter 6, we talked about the thinking distortion of taking things personally. The tendency to do this is especially strong when the criticism comes from you. Always remember, you are not an event. You may have done something stupid; that does not make you stupid, it makes you human. A child who has emptied the toy cupboard or trampled the teddy of a younger brother is not bad, vicious or naughty. They have done a naughty thing. They are a child.

And there is the difference between harsh and personal. I (BW) am really lucky to have a relationship with my daughter in which we often critique each other's work. We spend a long time red penning (or the online equivalent) the various bits of writing and sending them back. Someone once glanced at a piece I was about to send and was horrified, saying that I couldn't possibly be so brutal. But it is not brutal unless there is brutality involved. Both of us want nothing except for the other to be as good and successful as possible. And it is exactly the same with the way you critique yourself. Once you have stepped away from the personal, the self-damning, you will find that you can genuinely critique yourself on a deeper more valuable level. Once it no longer destroys you, every bit of criticism is an immense opportunity, whether it comes from you or someone else.

Positive Affirmation

One of the most effective tools to use to build and reinforce your Positive Self-Image is Positive Affirmation, mentioned earlier in the chapter. The premise is to create a positive statement about yourself – the 'I can's' of your new belief system– and speak it out loud.

Positive Affirmation has been used as part of a commitment to change across ages, continents and cultures. Now, with the development of neuroscience, we know that it is a form of gentle self-hypnosis, the results of which can be evidenced in the same way as a visualisation by means of an MRI scanner. It works best if you bring your imagination into play, if you're fully engaged in the process. Rather than repeating 'I love spiders' 30 times as a mere chant without ever thinking about a spider, try to imagine the spiders, imagine loving the spiders, feel and believe that you love the spiders!

It is likely that we have all filled a good percentage of our time in the past with negative affirmations, critical statements about ourselves that we have repeated again and again. These may vary from the very serious 'I hate myself' to the less serious 'I hate my bottom, my stomach, etc.', which can seem just as serious at the time. They may be statements that relate to the Big I that you wrote down in the last exercise. They may be statements that were once said to you, perhaps as a child, or they may be monsters of your own creation. Each time you have repeated them to yourself they have become more deeply reinforced.

Now is the time to disempower these negative statements as well as create positive affirmative ones. The first thing is to recognise them. If you have one or two Big I's, you'll be amazed how many times they come into your mind each day. Keep a sheet of paper handy and write them down. Some people prefer to keep them separate from their notebook, but it is up to you. And as they arrive, smile. Smile as if it is someone else having that absurdly ridiculous thought. If you find this impossible, try disempowering the statement in stages. If you habitually think 'I hate myself', change it to 'I dislike myself' to 'I'm OK' to 'I like myself' to 'I love myself'. And, of course, as you challenge and change your negative beliefs, these negative statements will become increasingly empty and will seem genuinely absurd and ridiculous.

Exercise 7.4: Positive Affirmation

Write out three Positive Affirmations that you will start to use on a daily basis. They are statements that apply to the you that you want to be. These can be practical or more abstract, whichever suits you best. It can be 'I love spiders!' or it can be 'My dreams are becoming reality. I am made of the stuff of stars!' But keep the language positive, no double negative's: 'I love spiders' rather than 'I am not afraid of spiders'. If you imagine this latter statement, the emotion that will come into your mind and body is fear.

Say each Positive Affirmation over and over for two minutes each, at some point in the day. It can be done when you are walking to the station or waiting for the train, but it is best if you are somewhere where you can fully commit to the process of saying them out loud. Try to engage with every fibre of your body and with the full focus of your mind. And, if they still feel unreal, don't worry, the more you embed them, the more 'real' they will feel. The more you use them to power the change that you are making to your life, the more they will apply to the you that you become.

Compassion and Self-Compassion

Closely tied to self-image and self-value is self-compassion. It's probably just worth noting that none of these concepts is born from self-centredness or from self-pity. So you have no reason to feel guilty about bringing your attention to yourself. It is simply developing a level of mindfulness, of awareness of yourself and learning not to judge. It is noticing how you 'speak' to yourself, the generosity of spirit with which you set your expectations and how seriously you take note of your dreams.

In fact, although many of us treat ourselves more harshly than we treat others, very few people treat themselves entirely differently from the way they treat other people, so compassion and self-compassion are pretty tightly bound at the hip. Those for whom compassion and self-compassion belong in different realities are those who, sadly, are suffering from some kind of narcissistic personality disorder and are literally unable to picture a world that does not orbit around them.

With both compassion and self-compassion, active engagement is required. We have to work hard to make sure that others do not suffer and it is the same with ourselves.

> **Exercise 7.5: Unconditional Self-Acceptance**
>
> Look at the negative statement from the Big I exercise earlier in this chapter and then close your eyes for a minute or two. Imagine that your best friend has come to you saying that this statement applies to them. They are distraught and realise that it is something they must address if they are to move on with their life.
>
> The next step is to write them a letter, explaining that you understand, that you love them anyway, and know that, with whatever support is needed, it will be alright.
>
> The final step, of course, is to go through the letter and make the changes needed for it to be a letter to yourself. Change all the you's to I or me, change any statements of phrases as needed to make it sound real. And then read it out loud.

Compassion is a close relative of empathy, which we will look at in the chapter on emotions. Most of us have a very high level of empathy with those who are close to us. We can, very often, accept the vulnerable, 'the child,' in our closest friends and be there to nurture and support. It is much harder to accept that vulnerable child in ourselves. It reminds us too soundly of the times when we were scared, in real or imagined danger, when we were the child in an adult world and we knew, absolutely knew, that there were monsters under the bed.

Sometimes, at the courses, when we talk about compassion and self-compassion, we are asked if we are really talking about love. It's a hard one to answer. In the West, our concept of love is primarily romantic, two-person focussed and often sentimentalised. But, of course, there are infinite kinds of love. Close your eyes, just for a moment, and imagine what the world would be without it. And, actually, it's not an ethereal or idealistic concept – we love our children, our dogs, our telly, our traditions and our takeaways on the way home from the pub!

Through the book, we have asked you to set goals around what you love to do and the *you* you would love to be. In the next section, when we ask you to think of the things you are grateful for, you will be thinking about the things and the people that you love in your life. So perhaps compassion and self-compassion are about being kind to yourself and to others and, for most people, the positive emotion that underpins this compassion will be love. It will, almost certainly, be closely aligned to the meaning you have thought about over the last few chapters. If it is this important, then we must surely choose what we love wisely. As far as you possibly can, love what is good for you and not what is bad for you.

The seventeenth-century Japanese saying, 'See no evil, hear no evil, speak no evil' implies that we should act only with positive generous compassion. Consider that just for a moment. Think, then, about how often we gossip or talk badly of people in a single day. On the level of neuroscience, this applies also to our thoughts. If we 'think evil', we are filling our brains with negatives, imagined or real, to which our mind, body and emotions will respond. This means that the act of compassion is self-compassion. And the opposite, of course, is also true.

The final note on compassion comes from science. When we anticipate eating a bar of chocolate or drinking a glass of wine, the pleasure hit comes largely from a release of the chemical dopamine. We are likely to get a much larger hit from an act of generosity or compassion. It seems that those through the ages who said that kindness is the way to find happiness have been proved right.

Gratitude

Gratitude is very closely related to our sense of wonder and, very simply, stops us from being dissatisfied. It is impossible to be actively engaged in the act of gratitude and to be thinking negative thoughts at the same time. I (BW) think of gratitude as an ANT repellent. If a negative thought presses itself into my mind and a mindfulness exercise won't expel it, I bring to mind the things I'm grateful for and, without exception, it wanders off. Sometimes, I'll do an Image Breathing exercise holding as the image something for which I am profoundly grateful – my daughter, the roof over my head, being able to teach and write about Mind Fitness. How many thousands of things every single day do we take for granted? We flick a switch and a light comes on, we turn on the kettle and the water heats up. Thousands. Without touching on our relationships and our health. And, surely, we must be grateful for our wonderful brains and the way they work that means that we can make this journey.

The list of things to be grateful for is endless. Be grateful for today – for having today. Respond as if it was the first day of life, and then the last day of your life. Be grateful for getting older, not everyone has the privilege. Gratitude for nature is so important. Just go to the window and look at the sky. We so rarely look at the sky. A recent research study has shown that the benefits to mental health from a walk outdoors, immersing yourself in nature, last for about seven hours. Isn't that wonderful? And yet, somehow, it is not a surprise.

All the great prophets and the leaders of every belief system talk about gratitude. Every religion, ancient and modern, is based on the please and thank you, the prayer and the grace. And the wonderful thing is that, the more you start to say thank you (especially out loud), the more you will feel it. Gratitude is at the heart of mindfulness. In the same way as looking out for the colour blue will make the colour increasingly vibrant, with daily mindfulness practice the cup becomes more and more full. In a profound way, you are looking at the world with different eyes. And because of the way we now understand the brain, it makes perfect sense. The more grateful we feel, the more we think ourselves into a state of gratitude, the more able we are to act in such a way that will bring about the good things in life that will give us further cause to be grateful.

Exercise 7.6: Gratitude Journal

Write a list of things that you're grateful for.

As soon as you can, buy another book, even a special book, perhaps one that you would be proud to own and keep, and make it your Gratitude Journal. Write three or more things that you are grateful for at the end of every day.

Chapter Recap

For this recap exercise, we'd like you to just write out one positive thing that you are going to do in relation to each section of the chapter. Make sure you feel positive as you do the exercise. Do it when you have plenty of time. Sit by a window. Grab a cup of water or tea. Place a photo of someone you care about next to you.

▶ Optimism: _____

▶ Acceptance: _____

▶ Positive Affirmation: _____

▶ Self-Image: _____

▶ Compassion: _____

▶ Self-Compassion: _____

▶ Gratitude: _____

Questions and Answers

▶ **Can I get someone else to change their Self-Image?**

The first thing to accept is that we can't control anyone but ourselves; we can't make anyone do anything.

However, it's true that we have a profound effect on the thoughts and emotions of other people. It is likely that most people who have set out to teach or assist young people, for example, did not do so with the express intent of changing their pupil's Self-Image. But they almost certainly have. There are so many ways that we can help others to feel good about themselves. One is, as we have said, by giving praise, by simply commenting on something that has been done well.

If you have the time, you can offer to be a guide or mentor if someone wants consciously to enter a process of change. But make sure that you are helping them to help themselves. Resilience not reliance. Keep a check that you are not creating a dependence that would send their Self-Image flying backwards if the relationship was to end.

▶ **Is seeing the Little I's instead of the Big I about forgiving yourself?**

Identifying the Little I's is about searching your life for genuinely positive qualities and attributes that you have, and positive actions that you take or have taken in the past. It is about recognising the good that is already there and needs to be placed in a more important position in your life.

But perhaps *seeing* the Little I's, really seeing them and not the Big I when you look at the page may require you to forgive yourself, yes. Just remember that you are not any one action that you have done. Nor are you any one quality or emotion that has come to dominate your life. You need to face any monsters down. There are hardly any of us alive that don't have them. Look at the big picture, Big I and Little I's until they become integrated into a whole, wonderful, flawed human being.

That unconditional self-acceptance and integration is the path to forgiveness and a vital part of nurturing a healthy Self-Image.

Conclusion

Be aware of your Self-Image and do all that you can to make it strong. Recognise your strengths and successes and do all you can to actively bring about change in the way you see yourself. Perhaps the biggest secret of self-worth is to appreciate other people more. Think about what this might mean for you. Join a local community group, volunteer for something you believe in or visit an elderly relative you haven't seen for a while. Give praise whenever you can. By doing so, you can turn around someone's day, occasionally their lives.

And, remember, every negative thought about someone else you conceive damages you. All the techniques in this book will move you slowly from acting generously to thinking generously. Try to act and think only with positive compassion. It sounds impossible. Of course it is, you are a fallible human being; you have to course-correct. Sometimes, you'll have to course-correct a lot! And that's OK. But hold it in your mind, remind yourself of it when you need to. Think and act only with positive compassion.

Never play the sympathy card, a difficult one for many of us to get out of. Instead, let every word and action express the confidence that you are on your way, moving in the right direction, with so much to be grateful for.

You have set goals based on your beliefs and meaning and they have determined your path. Gradually, as you live more in the moment, as you have more confidence in your ability to course-correct, your life will become more about the journey than the destination. Not only will you be headed towards a place that is beautiful and full of wonder, but you will enjoy everything that you pass and take part in along the way.

CHAPTER

8

Get in tune with your body

How to use your body to reduce stress and perform at your best

Unlike many cognitive therapies and courses, Mind Fitness is designed to encompass the body, to look at the ways that we can use our new thinking skills to feel more comfortable in our skins and, now, using new science, to look at ways that we can employ our wonderful bodies to help us on the journey towards a grounded, authentic you.

In every part of the Mind Fitness process there are a myriad of physical functions that are engaged. As we have said before, each one of us is an electrochemical organism and every change that occurs in our brain ripples out into an almost infinite number of places in our body. And let's not forget that, if we are working towards being happier, there is a lot of pleasure to be derived from physical sensation, and from our ability to move through space and time in our complex and ever changing 'dance'.

In that dance, we are not alone, but rather we are interacting with those both close to us and far away, on a physical as well as a mental and emotional plane. Of course, our arms go out to hold our child when he cries, our body seeming to feel his need in an intense and even painful way, but it goes far deeper than that. We know now that our bodies move to be in tune with others. We often move to mirror another in an intimate conversation or when we feel a need to be in tune, perhaps in an interview or important meeting. We breathe more deeply as we watch an athlete run as fast as they can, and a collection of muscles will engage if we watch someone give birth. It is why sports such as football can make us feel so totally immersed; we can be mentally, emotionally and even physically engaged.

The Mind Body Problem

Pre-neuroscience, the big question that had been argued over for centuries was, 'Are we a body with a mind or a mind with a body?' Is there some non-physical part of you that could live outside the body? The philosopher Descartes[1] famously contested that the mind and body were separate entities that, even if all physical sensations were an illusory dream, our mind would still exist, stating, 'I think therefore I am'. He would have come down firmly on the side of 'A mind with a body.'

Now, because of neuroscience, most scientists reject the idea of separation. We know that there is a continuous, complex, sometimes even tangled relationship between body and mind. It is worth remembering, of course, that we are constantly assessed by others as a physical being. Some psychologists even believe that our personalities mould to our appearance because that is the way we are treated by others. If we look aggressive or sly, for example, we may be treated as someone who embodies these traits and then gradually take them on. Of course, if we are aware of this (as you are now much more likely to be), we can counter the effect with the processes described through this book.

Exercise 8.1: Awareness of Physicality

It's interesting to do a quick awareness exercise. Choose two people that you know reasonably well:

▶ Spend five minutes looking at a picture of each. From the picture alone (and this is hard if you know them well) what traits would you attribute to them? Try to be aware of your thought process in making your decisions.

▶ Then consider the way that others you know treat the two people. Make a quick list.

▶ Finally, jot down how far you think the two inhabit the characteristics you have attributed to them.

Over time, our personality adapts to our perception of the way that people are treating us. For example, many who have had to cope with a sudden physical disfigurement report a far greater change in people's treatment of them than is borne out by video evidence. They may then begin to act as if they are victims of discrimination.

The Mind and the Body as One

From the moment we are born, our bodies are deeply integrated with the activity in our brains to form what we call consciousness. Our mental development, in fact, is formed by our bodies' interaction with the external world. Every sight, sound and touch becomes a new map in the brain and we know now that, thanks to Neuroplasticity, this continues to be the case throughout the whole of our lives. Our bodies and external sensations are inseparable from our subjective consciousness – they are an integral part of the way we perceive the world and ourselves. Ancient Buddhist philosophers have long understood the integral mind-body relationship. They tell us that if we close our eyes the sensation of body does not melt away (as in the Descartes model) and, in fact, these sensations are central to the process of meditation.

Awareness of our Body

Most of us take our pretty amazing bodies for granted and, as we start to age, our relationship with our body can become something of a battle, if we let it.

So, first we are going to take a little time to concentrate just on awareness of our body. All the focus work we have done will help us, and this honing in on our physical form will, in turn, develop our ability to focus. And, for some, there is a real feeling of 'coming home' as mind and body start to work more closely with each other, perhaps not dissimilar to the feeling we get when we bring goals, belief and meaning into one composite whole.

Exercise 8.2: Body Scan

For this exercise it is best to lie down if you can.

Get yourself comfortable with your arms either by your side or resting gently on your stomach. Begin by being aware, for a moment, of any parts of your body that are in contact with the floor. Now, take two deep breaths, breathing in through your nose and out through your mouth, and then close your eyes.

We'll start by being aware of the breath, as before, but concentrating on what changes occur in the body because of the breath and through the breath. Bring your awareness to the rise and fall of your rib cage. Don't try to change the way you breathe in any way, just be aware of it exactly as it is.

Again, as we are working through the exercise, if other thoughts come into your mind, notice them and then let them drift away, bringing your attention back to the physical sensations. We're going to work slowly through the body. You may find this a very relaxing exercise but that isn't the objective; the object is simply awareness. We will start at the feet and work our way up to the head.

Bring your attention to the toes of both feet, concentrate on any sensations you can feel. If you have bare feet, what does the air feel like as it makes contact with

---

your toes? Some people report a sensation of heat or even tingling as they bring their attention to one single part of the body. But, if you feel nothing at all, that's fine too, just note the fact. As you become more practised at the Mind Fitness exercises you'll be able to simply feel the physical sensations rather than analyse them, but, at this stage, analyse away!

Move your attention now to the rest of your feet, focussing for a moment on the working of your ankle and at the place where muscle and ligaments meet bone. Are the sensations the same in each foot or slightly different?

Bring your focus now up to your calf muscles, often a place in which a sizeable amount of tension resides. Move your attention around the front of your legs to the shins and up to the knees. Sometimes, as your attention travels up your body, you will discover little pockets of pain; make a mental note of these too.

Bring your attention to the thighs and to the back of the legs, and then to the buttocks and pelvis. As well as thoughts that come into your mind, make a mental note of any emotions that suddenly appear, and then gently bring your focus back.

Move your attention to your hips and to your stomach. Again, be aware of how your stomach connects with your breath. Take your attention to the chest, being aware of the way that your rib cage envelops your vital organs, focussing on the back and sides as well as the ribs at the front.

Move your attention to your shoulders and upper arms. Note any tension that you are carrying. How exactly does this feel? For some, there may be a sense of quite profound relief or release. Then move your attention slowly down each arm, front and back, until you get to your wrists; be particularly aware of the joints, the pivotal path of the working physical frame.

Take your focus into your hands, letting it rest for a moment on the muscle group between thumb and wrist. Then bring your attention to your knuckles and then into your fingers, either one at a time or together as you find best.

Move the attention, when you are ready, back up each arm and, once again, into the shoulders. Is the sensation the same as it was when you rested here before or has it changed?

Move your focus now into your neck, front and back, into your jaw. This, again, is an area where you are likely to encounter tension, and then up into your cheeks, temples, eyes and forehead and, finally, into the back of your head.

Now move back to concentrating on the breath. Take a moment to note any significant thoughts that come into your mind or, perhaps, any emotions. Then open your eyes.

It's good to go slowly when you do a Body Scan for the first time, but it is an exercise that can fit around your timetable and needs. It can take an hour or it can take a minute.

Take a moment to jot down in your notebook any recurring thoughts, unexpected emotions or areas of the body where you encountered tension or resistance.

Many people find a Body Scan a good exercise to mark the transition from work life to home life. It's also a great one to do before a period of physical exercise, just before you run or begin an exercise class.

You will have noticed the increase in sensations as you focussed on each part of your body. This increase in sensation 'wakes up' your mind.

When you do the Body Scan a second time, focus on any energy that you can feel pulsing through – is it tingly, vibrating, pulsing? Is it warm or cool? Is it heavy or light?

As we said, you become more experienced and your awareness deepens, let yourself become immersed in the physical experience. Try to move away from consciously acknowledging and analysing a sensation to simply experiencing it.

Exercise 8.3: The Feet

Mindfulness practitioners will often ask you to place your feet flat on the floor, even when you are sitting, to help you get the feeling of being grounded. Certainly, the feet play an important part in the sensation of being centred.

1   Stand in a comfortable position with your feet shoulder width apart. Feel the energy dropping through you with gravity towards the floor, until it is centred in your feet. Spend two minutes experiencing this swell around your ankles and feet, and then concentrate for one more minute on the feeling of each foot's connection with the floor. Imagine the energy moving through the feet into the floor, grounding you.

2   Walk for two minutes somewhere; where it is practical and comfortable do so with bare feet. As you walk, register each tiny sensation that occurs as your weight moves through each of your feet.

The Senses

Awareness will, as we have said, sharpen the experience provided by your senses. If we think about feeling happier, more vibrant, more alive, this heightened sensory perception is probably a good part of what we are imagining. I (BW) know that fairly soon after I began the Mind Fitness process I had a very clear feeling of having woken up, of having a different level of sensory awareness than I had had before. Many poets through the centuries have used the metaphor of senses 'dancing'.

In school, we were taught that we have five senses: sight, hearing, smell, touch and taste. In fact, there are a lot more. Neurologists typically work with between nine and twenty-one.[2] These include the perception of pressure, vibration, heat and pain. They also include our sense of balance and, most commonly, proprioception, the brain's knowledge of the relative position of body parts. They are worth investigation, if you are interested. Some animals have senses that we don't (as far as we currently know) and are able to sense electrical and magnetic fields, water pressure and currents. Perhaps choose one of these extra senses to focus on each day and just 'look' out for it. If it is perception of pressure, notice the levels of pressure in different people's hugs or handshakes, or the way your bag strap pushes into your shoulder.

The Stress Hormones

How does what happens in our brain affect what happens in our body?

Perhaps the most common way is through the workings of the stress hormones adrenaline and cortisol, already talked about at various points in the book. While these are necessary when we are in real danger, they can be lethal when the fight or flight response is switched on all the time. Very quickly, the immune system begins to work less effectively (as the protection from the external threat is prioritised) and the healing process is slowed down. This is why we get sick as exams approach or as we come up to a pressurised time at work. In fact, the butterflies in the stomach feeling that we all know so well is blood vessels shutting down to look after the essential organs. As we have said before, in a state of fight or flight, no information gets fed up to the prefrontal cortex. It's why we, quite literally, go blank in exams or presentations. We have switched from creative thinking to reflex behaviour.

In addition, almost any health condition will be compounded by the anxiety you attach to it. If you worry about a problem, mental or physical, it will, almost certainly, get worse.

Our gut as second brain

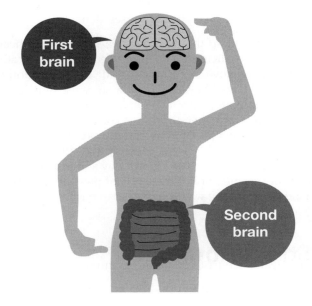

The Enteric Nervous System in our gut is a hub of intelligence. In fact, it is often referred to as our second brain, having, perhaps, the same number of neurons (about 200 million) as the brain of a dog.[3] This second 'brain' can react without consulting or communicating with our first brain. Think of all the sayings that bear this out:

- ▶ Gut reaction
- ▶ Gut instinct
- ▶ Gut-wrenching experience

There is a close interdependence between big brother and small brother; the two are constantly sending messages to each other and constantly making small changes and adjustments to the way the relationship is working. So, if you find yourself on the way to a deli, it could be that your stomach has just sent your brain a message to say that it is empty. Like the big brain, its objective is to keep you healthy, but, like the big brain, it will interpret this through the lens of your past experience. So, if instead you find yourself on the way to the chip shop, it's time to get a little more training in!

This relationship means that almost anything that is good for your brain is good for your gut and, therefore, your physical health. This is true for nutritional foods and for exercise as well as for mindfulness and adopting a positive approach to life.

Pain

Pain, as you might imagine, is both a physical and emotional experience and is affected by both the mind and body. It signals nerve damage or damage to tissues but can also be a warning signal of potential damage.

Most of us know all too well that our experience of pain is affected by stress, anxiety and depression. It can, of course, also be affected by a positive, calm state of wellbeing. Mindfulness is now used extensively in the UK National Health Service as part of programmes constructed for controlling pain, and it is proving a powerful and effective tool in the armoury.

Healing

We know that the body is capable of curing itself when directed by the mind and emotions. Scientists have known that this self-direction plays a role in recovery ever since they could measure that not all people recover at the same speed to the same condition (this is not the same with mice). There are also a plethora of reports of people being cured by placebo treatments, across a very wide range of conditions.[4]

More and more scientists are understanding that the role of the physician is to facilitate the body's inherent ability to heal itself. This is very much in line with the Mind Fitness process where we look to build resilience not reliance and give people the tools to look after their own mental health. As a species, we are programmed for survival – both brain and body will work towards this if they are given a fighting chance. Many complimentary treatments are based on this principle; osteopathy works by ensuring that the musculoskeletal system is in alignment and obstructions to blood and lymph glands are minimised or eliminated.

Of course, there are times when serious medical conditions need pharmaceutical or surgical intervention but, even in serious conditions, we can help ourselves to recover by minimising the stress we add to the situation. Rapid healers across a multitude of tests are optimistic, positive thinkers who expect to get well quickly and have something to get well for.

Physical Exercise

As we have said, physical and mental health go together. What is good for your muscles is good for your brain. There is a range of benefits to brain health that devolve from exercising the body. Exercise improves the ability of the brain cells to grow and develop, and releases powerful endorphins that give us a sense of wellbeing and help us to regulate emotions. Conversely, a lack of exercise is a recognised contributory factor in cases of depression and anxiety.

The best time to exercise is in the morning as early exercise increases the brain's ability to handle stress through the day. In some cases, it triples. For most of us, willpower is also highest at the beginning of the day. We would say, though, that the most important thing is to choose a form of exercise that you love.

Getting great sleep

All the exercises and reframing that you do as you work through this book will help you to sleep better. Cognitive Behavioural Treatment for Insomnia (CBTI) is now the most effective method for sleep problems, having superseded medication as the treatment that works better for most people.[5]

We all have a difficult night's sleep from time to time. The problem comes when we get used to thinking that it's normal that we aren't sleeping so well because we're stressed. And, as chronic stress becomes the norm, we forget what a good night's sleep felt like.

Of course, the more we worry about not sleeping, the harder it becomes and the semi-conscious space is an easy one for the ANTs to invade. But we can't be complacent. A good sleep pattern is an important ingredient in good mental health and a lot of housekeeping, preparation and recovery takes place as we sleep. If you are having problems sleeping, try doing the Body Scan (see page 108) but gently tensing and releasing each body part as you move through. Make sure you are getting enough fresh air, drinking enough water and keep tech out of the bedroom, if you possibly can.

Most importantly, work on reframing your unhelpful beliefs and Thinking Errors to dissipate the root cause of the stress. In fact, we would say do all of this, even if you drop off easily. Great sleep is not just about falling asleep quickly or getting enough. We go through a series of stages of sleep each night; each is necessary if we are to feel our best and perform at our potential.

Relaxation

You can use physical relaxation to control an emotional response. If your muscles are completely relaxed, it is impossible to feel an emotion of anger, frustration or fear. If you feel the approach of one of these emotions and you aren't able to think yourself down, you can use a calm body to acquire a calm mind.

Building time for relaxation into your new Mind Fitness regime is really important. There are a full range of benefits from being able to relax – from improved mood and motivation to improved sleep, higher levels of focus and energy, and improved memory. It doesn't have to be doing nothing or sitting in front of the television. It can be getting creative, listening to music, walking or exploring the mindfulness exercises. Anything that you know will not result in you feeling pressure or having to battle off the ANTs.

Of course, the whole Mind Fitness course will help you to relax more easily and more deeply and all the mindfulness exercises will mean that you're pretty expert in bringing your attention to the physical sensations of your body and resting in the breath. In fact the body has a natural ease, so again it is about finding this, about learning to get out of your own way. Once the body and mind have assumed their natural ease it is simply being alert to any thoughts that might disturb this.

Ageing

As we know from Chapter 3 (Neuroplasticity) dementia involves a build-up on the synapses, which causes them eventually to break down. Making sure that you are creating new neural pathways through new ideas and new learning is key to keeping your brain healthy.

It's also just worth mentioning that, in the same way that stress is about our *perceived* ability to cope, ageing also involves a substantial measure of perception. It's not about whether your coping skills are up to the job, but whether you think they are.

It is the direction in which you are headed that counts; keep setting and re-setting goals. Visualise yourself as someone who has a youthful energy, who likes to explore and to learn and who embraces change. And keep hold of your meaning. We have all seen the detrimental effect when someone gives up work and doesn't replace it with something that gives them a sense of purpose.

If you think about it, age itself is a matter of perception. A medieval man or woman would have considered themselves old at 50. If a medication was introduced next year that kept everyone alive and immensely healthy to 200, we would quickly feel old at 201. We already choose the age we feel in so many ways, but, for many of us, that is a negative and debilitating, or at least, limiting process. It doesn't have to be. It's never too late to breathe new life into your life.

Using our Body for Better Mental Health

If we have accepted that the chemicals that move constantly through our body have a direct impact on everything down to the structure of the body's cells, it is then about how much we can be in control of that release, and whether we can employ the body itself to help in the process. And it seems that we can. Almost everything works in both directions – our mind affects our body and our body affects our mind. Our thoughts affect our emotions and our emotions affect our thoughts. Which means that we can choose to intervene wherever works best for us. And, in terms of the body, the more you get in touch, in tune with it through the mindfulness techniques, the easier it becomes to use it as a tool to help you become calmer and more confident.

We all understand how body language works. We know that a significant aspect of communication is non-verbal. We are constantly 'reading' other people's thoughts, feelings and intentions through their body language and, of course, they are doing the same to us. People who have high emotional intelligence are often very good at reading the signs. It's called kinesics.

Getting good at it is largely about awareness. We all know that crossed arms and legs read as resistance, bad posture as apathy, no eye contact betrays a lie and fake smiles don't crinkle the eyes – but it's whether or not we are picking up on this that counts. Using the example of poor posture – it's not whether it's good or bad that counts, but how it reads. How do we interpret it? Getting good at reading body language can improve communications, help relationships run more smoothly and ease our progress through most paths in life.

Exercise 8.4: Reading Body Language

Each day, pick one person, a stranger, and really look at their body language. Someone on a bus or train is good. Start with a broad sweep; how are they holding themselves? Are they open or closed? And then really hone in on the detail. Notice the little gestures. What do they tell you about the person? Trust your instinct. We are, most of us, better at reading body language than we realise. But be honest with yourself – we can also make sweeping judgements and assumptions from body language.

Our own body language, then, is incredibly important. We have said that people respond to the way that they are treated; it's also true that the way that we are treated depends on the way people are perceiving us because of our body language. If we stoop and wring our hands, people will be reading this as insecurity and anxiety. If they are treating us as someone who is insecure and anxious, then very quickly this will be how we feel. Most body language is unconscious. It is really important to become aware of yours.

This would be important enough, but neuroscience tells us that it goes further. Our brain actually reads our own body language, in just the same way as it reads that of another person, and delivers up the appropriate chemicals and emotions.

The ground-breaking studies were conducted by Amy Cuddy, who, with her partner Dana Carnie, coined the term 'Power Poses.'[6]

Power Poses

We can use our bodies to make us feel more powerful, more able to cope. Our bodies can, quite literally, change our minds. As Cuddy stresses, it isn't faking it til you make it – it's faking it until you become it.

Exercise 8.5: Power Poses

Stand in a Power Pose – the key is openness, so perhaps arms up in the common sportsman's triumph pose, or widely settled on your hips, feet slightly apart. Within about two minutes, your body will flood with adrenalin and testosterone. You will feel more powerful. You will behave in a way that reflects this.

Now stand in a position that disempowers you, perhaps arms closed in around you, feet together, head down. Within two minutes, your body will flood with the stress hormone cortisol. You will feel anxious and less able to cope.

The implications of this are huge. In tests, Cuddy and Carnie sent test subjects who had done both poses into job interviews and those who had done the High Power Pose far exceeded expectations. (Please note that this means doing the pose before the interview, not during it!) The opposite was true for those who did the disempowering pose. The results have meant that many organisations (and political parties) have built them into their regular programmes of training.

Tiny tweaks are enough to start the process of big change. It simply makes sense to engage your body as friend and ally and, at the same time, deepen the process of seeing 'you' as a wonderfully complex whole.

Questions and Answers

▶ **Does having rituals that you perform before you go to bed help you sleep?**

It depends on what the ritual is; always taking your phone into bed and checking emails would not be good. But as long as they are rituals that help your body and brain to cleanse and relax, then yes. It is about preparing; you are preparing your mind for rest. And it is about building habits and neural pathways. If you know that you have a certain routine and then sleep soundly, it will become an embedded pattern, the most used route.

▶ **I find it much more relaxing to potter round the house, is this OK?**

Yes, absolutely. Sometimes, it is when we are determined to relax and sit still that our mind is quickly overrun with ANTs. Giving your brain something simple to occupy it may prevent this from happening. And, if pottering means uncluttering, then that has its own built-in benefits.

But anything can be relaxing, for example reading a book or watching a TV programme. The reason why this has stopped being the respite that it was is that we often now do other things while watching the TV – looking at social media, emails and so on. Try, as we've said, to do one thing at a time. It's so much better for mental health.

Conclusion

Our relationship with our body, or perhaps more accurately our 'oneness', is particularly important at this time when we are considering future technologies such as neural prosthetics, implants and wearable robots that could become an extended part of 'us'. The Mind/Body question moves up to a whole other level.

From what we now know of the adaptability of our body and brain, it is even possible that, by extending our sense of self to new wearable devices, our brains may adapt to accommodate a restructured version of self with new sensory representations. In other words, we may start to sense and have 'feeling' in these new extended parts of us.

We already have to accept a new set of responsibilities that come from understanding that our biological future is not solely determined by our genes. We know now that our genes respond to our environment. Signals come in from the external world. Your brain responds to the world and then sends chemistry into the blood. This controls the behaviour and genetics of your cells. It is called Signal Transduction. What environment they respond to is largely up to us. Some see this as being as empowering as the discovery of neuroplasticity. But it means we have to work harder to clear our cognitive bias because otherwise the cells will be responding to messages and beliefs that we have not chosen to guide our life.

What's most important is that we choose to look after our body and, in doing so, look after our mind. We can choose to eat well, drink enough, get enough sleep, exercise and relax. We can also choose to help our body by thinking well, by not allowing the ANTs to lead us down the spiral of negative thought and worry. Research is tying the relationship between mind and body ever more tightly. We aren't fully aware of the impact of, say, an outburst of anger. But the relationship is something we must embrace rather than fear because the positive potential is enormous. Our minds can help us to be more in tune with our bodies and our bodies can help us to be more positive, to be fully engaged and to reap more pleasure from our lives.

9

Unleash your imagination

Learn to power your Creativity and use it in your daily life

> We act or fail to act not because of will as is so commonly believed but because of imagination.
>
> Dr Maxwell Maltz[1]

By this point in the book, you have already employed your imagination in a wide range of exercises. Sometimes, when we're running the course, we have someone who is worried when they hear that imagination is used throughout because they don't see themselves as creative. A handful of people have even told us 'but I have no imagination'.

As you have become familiar with the way the mind works, you may have noted that, for most people, our imagination actually plays a huge part in the negative emotions that can dominate our lives. It is what we do as we self-talk, when we perceive a danger that may not be there. It is what we do when we perceive ourselves as weak, incompetent, overweight. Our brain is showing us an image of this negative version of us. Mind Fitness uses the imagination to undertake the same process but in reverse – to visualise a competent and successful you and then guide your brain to make this your new neural pathway.

We have long known the importance of the imagination in driving invention and social change. Even Napoleon said, 'Imagination rules the world.'[2] Creativity is sometimes called the bridge to innovation. In order to create something new, an inventor has to be able first to imagine it, whether this is a piece of kitchen equipment or an equation. Most scientists and mathematicians say that imagination lies at the heart of their work. Similarly, a concert pianist practises in his mind; he also composes there. Now, with our understanding of neuroscience, we know why imagination rules the world. We know that it drives not only social change but all change; it is imagination that is enabling you to successfully reframe your thoughts and unlock your potential.

In the first half of this chapter, we'll reinforce some of the concepts and techniques from previous chapters that have used imagination. The second half of the chapter will be a comprehensive set of exercises to sharpen your creative skills and to use imagination to bring about further positive change.

What is Imagination? What is Creativity?

Imagination is a private individual activity. Creativity is the outward expression of imagination. Having said that, imagination is also what we use to immerse ourselves in the social world. We spend a huge amount of time using our imagination to read the emotions of other people. It is what engages us in any story or situation. Have a look at a TV drama or movie and see how much of the camera time is given to close-ups. Whether in real life or if we are being an 'audience' (which actually demands a substantial creative output), we want to share in the emotions of others and to do this we use our imagination.

As we said in the Foreword, scientists used to believe that there was very little connection between the imagination and the prefrontal cortex, the higher thinking brain. Now it is known that the links are incredibly strong. As with most connections, it works in both directions; this is called bio-directionality. You can use your imagination to develop your focus and power of concentration and you can use focussed thought to encourage and facilitate moments of creative insight.

When you have one of these creative moments, perhaps an idea or realisation (sometimes referred to as an 'aha' moment), your brain and autonomic nervous system shut down just for a fraction of a second.[3] All 'power' is concentrated into the insight. Isn't that amazing? It also means that your increased ability to focus through doing the work in this book will enable you to have many more of these creative moments. For experienced meditators, it becomes a state they can call up at will.

Our imagination isn't centred in one part of the brain. In fact, when we use our 'imagination', over 40 different areas of the brain are used. New ideas come from new connections, when neurons fire and wire together. If we asked you to close your eyes and think of a pink elephant, you would be able to see one, although your brain cannot draw upon a memory of you having seen such a wonderful beast. That is because your brain can take familiar pieces and assemble them in a different way. There will be an ensemble of neurons that would collectively call up the image of an elephant and others that would be used to visualise the colour pink. You can even add in that this elephant is wearing a crown and waltzing. The really clever part of this mental synthesis is that each ensemble of neurons will take a different amount of time to fire, but the brain can balance this out so that there is a unified conduction time and the elephant does not have to wait to go pink or begin to dance.

Think of it as being like an orchestra finding new sounds and combinations, new ways of expressing a thought or story. Creativity, then, is linked to the ability to make new connections so, the more we are accustomed to using adaptive behaviour, to constant new learning and embracing change, the more active our imagination.

The more imagination we can employ, the better our abilities to solve problems, to listen with attention and to course-correct. Of course, it is not just 'creatives' who need these skills. What artists and performers do, we all do all the time. We are all creative beings.

How Mind Fitness employs Imagination

You are the creator of your own life so being the best you can be at creating it is very important. Now that you've got the hang of challenging unhelpful beliefs and managing your response to external events, you are, to a large extent, making up your story. Your imagination will help choose the story you want this to be.

Our imagination can help us through the most difficult periods in life. Because of Neuroplasticity we know that we are what we think about most. It requires enormous strength to think positively when surrounded by extreme negativity, but, thanks to our abilities to reason and to imagine, it can be done.

Imagination is also an important means to hold our meaning clear and strong, particularly when this is challenged. Think about the amazing work of people like Mother Teresa or Viktor Frankl whose *Man's Search for Meaning* we mentioned early in the book. Imagination allows us to visualise forward, to see a better future and set our course in that direction. And it is our imagination that enables us to feel compassion for others, to empathise and, from that, to seek to make a difference.

Adaptive Behaviour and creativity are very closely linked. As an artist, you are always working in the moment, in response to another person or an external stimulus. If you have a friend you can work with, there's an excellent creative adaptive exercise you can do. You place a sheet of A4 or A3 blank paper between you and each take a pencil. You then draw a picture, each of you taking turns to work on the drawing for a minute at a time. Try to use what the other person has drawn so you are continually reframing and replanning creatively.

There are many other benefits of a strong and active imagination. Those who habitually employ creativity are likely to be more secure when taking risks, more open minded and more receptive to new experience. They are likely to be able to think laterally or 'outside the box' and to be effective team workers. These are all qualities we have been working to strengthen through the book. And it works both ways – throughout the book the exercises you are doing will be strengthening your imagination. For example, as you work on reducing your cognitive bias you will be creating a more open mind. While cognitive bias blocks creativity because it imposes limits and dictates places that your thoughts cannot go, clearing that bias will release untapped creative potential. Your mindfulness work will, for example, induce a state where you are alert but relaxed; it is in that state where we are most likely to have an inspired thought, a hunch, so again creative potential will be released.

The role of the subconscious in rational thought is still being researched. A number of great thinkers and inventors have sworn by the process of setting their subconscious mind a task and giving it the time to come up with the solution while not thinking consciously about it. Isaac Newton's wife said that if her husband was stuck on any part of a problem he would simply take a nap and wait for the solution to arrive. Thomas Edison would enter a near sleep state, having given his subconscious something to work on, while holding a ball. As he fell asleep, he would drop the ball, suddenly waking to write down all that he had imagined. Many artists say that they feel the creativity moving 'through' them and that, when they achieve this creative state, the music or poetry writes itself.

Scientists are also looking at the link between memory and imagination. We know now that a single memory is held in many different parts of the brain and that memories are rewritten each time we visit them. This means that the present influences the past as well as the other way round. Think, if you can, of a memory that you have that has changed substantially over time. It is common when we bring to mind a person who has passed away. We often highlight or exaggerate their positive qualities while anything more negative is gradually erased from the memories we have of them. A developed imagination and creativity will serve you well in preserving your memories into old age. Similarly, nurturing the skill of memorising develops the imagination.

Perhaps, most importantly, in the context of this book, we can use our imagination to power our journey towards the sense of happiness and wellbeing. The promotion of neural connections involved in creativity emits the neurotransmitter serotonin, the chemical that produces the feeling of deep happiness and contentment. Both dopamine and serotonin also lubricate the passage to the higher thinking brain, so, again, the benefit works both ways. And a more optimistic outlook developed through the Mind Fitness process means that you are using your imagination in a constructive and positive way.

The Imagination and Self-Image

Not surprisingly, our ability to change our Self-Image depends very largely on a creative approach. Self-Image is, essentially, the way we see or imagine ourselves. As we said, in the section on Self-Image in Chapter 7, many people are literally hypnotised, programmed by a negative Self-Image. They are responding appropriately to the demands of this Self-Image and moving further into the negative spiral. When you change your Self-Image by cultivating helpful beliefs, you are providing your brain with a new truth. The better we are at imagining this new truth, the more effectively we are able to do this.

When you are working on your Self-Image, give yourself the time to really imagine. If it helps, develop an outline or skeleton of the aspect of yourself you are envisioning, then gradually 'colour' it in. Give it tones, textures. Imagine the detail. For example, if you are working on the positive affirmation that you are someone who does not panic in a situation, you might do this in various stages:

▶ Imagine the situation, be specific

▶ See your broad actions – I do this, I move here, I say this

▶ Now go in and consider the finer actions, a smile, a pause. Imagine what you are noticing

▶ Then go in and fill in the physiology and emotions – how exactly am I feeling and how is this affecting me?

And, as you build this new Self-Image, make sure a good dollop of creativity is in the mix. Imagine the kind of creativity you would like to have and to use. This, in turn, will power your continued change.

Creativity and Healing

There is sound evidence that creative therapies, sometimes called expressive therapies, that centre on drama, dance, music and art, can be highly effective in the treatment of depression, anxiety, phobia and some forms of psychosis.

The art forms are used to:-

▶ Solve problems

▶ Explore truths about the self

▶ Understand recurring images

▶ Explore unhealthy patterns of behaviour

▶ Come to terms with difficult situations

There is a long history of the arts as a positive part of the healing rituals of many ancient societies. Today, drama therapy, art therapy, music therapy and dance therapy are all used widely within the health system.

For those that work in the creative industries, it is no surprise that current science is validating the enormous benefit that everyone has known about for more than 50 years, or 5,000, if you include the ancient traditions. Certainly, there is enough evidence to advise every reader to go away and create! If you can do it as part of a group – there are some excellent community drama groups and community choirs – so much the better.

Creative Exercises

In the same way that we can visualise an end goal or a way to solve a problem, we can imagine an emotion. You'll have noticed that, if you feel bad, either physically or emotionally, but have to go into a situation where it's hard to let this show, you will often end up feeling a lot better. (This can work the opposite way when your negative emotion is very strong and the mere pretence of being 'fine' stacks up an extra layer of tension.) Similarly, if any of you have ever pulled a 'sickie' at work, the ironic result is that, by the time you've described the symptoms to two or three people, you're often feeling less than your best!

So, when you are using your imagination in any of these exercises, try to build emotion into the mix. If you are imagining yourself having achieved that ultimate goal, then build in the excitement and joy that you would feel. And remember to own the experience that you are visualising – hold the picture in the full faith that whatever you have imagined is yours. No humility is needed or required; play to win. Of course, you can't win by playing to lose; you also can't win by playing not to lose – think how often we fall into that trap.

Keep your visualisation work positive. If you feel it moving into something negative, gently bring it back. I (BW) sometimes do this with just a quick mental snapshot of a recent happy memory. The more you replay a visualisation, the more deeply the engrain beds in and, therefore, the more effective it becomes. So, if you find one of the exercises really works for you, try to repeat it often.

Start to build 'imagine if' into your life and your conversations. This can be based in reality to help promote change, such as 'imagine if my boss was the most compassionate of all employers'. Or it can be as abstract as you like, just to get you thinking outside the box. There's plenty of time waiting for a bus to imagine how the world would look if Santa was president or if your cat could suddenly talk!

Exercise 9.1: Visualisation of Scenario with Boss or Partner

Sit yourself comfortably, take one or two deep breaths, feel yourself centred and close your eyes.

Think of a scene between either you and your boss or you and your partner, which you know needs to play out. Perhaps it's something that you know you need to ask for but have been putting off. Or something that you weren't happy about, that you need, now that you are calm, to be spoken about, so that it doesn't happen again.

Imagine where this conversation will be taking place and where each of you is sitting or standing. Now play the scene through in your imagination – it shouldn't last more than one minute.

After the scene, look at how it went. Could it have gone better for you? If so, replay it, tweaking the responses to what you are saying so that it becomes more positive. Notice how differently you have to behave to make this happen.

Repeat the scene up to five times, each time acknowledging the different input from you.

Exercise 9.2: Using Imagination to Counter Negative Self-Talk

Next time you notice Negative Self-Talk creeping in, make a note of it.

Then imagine a critic standing behind you speaking these negative thoughts.

Now turn and confront this critic, countering each and every statement. If someone else were attacking you in this way, what would you say?

After the exercise, commit your counter attack to memory so that you can use it each time the Negative Self-Talk creeps in.

Exercise 9.3: Visualising a Difficult Task

This exercise is similar to a Goal-Based Visualisation.

First, pick a task or activity that you would find difficult in a public arena, for example a presentation. Next, imagine the speech you might deliver – two or three points is sufficient.

Then go through the presentation in your mind, imagining the most receptive audience ever, your family and very best friends. Imagine how positively they would respond.

Finally, gradually replace each member of your friendly audience with a person who is likely to be there if you know them, or random individuals if your presentation will be to strangers. Keep the positive response from these people exactly the same.

Whatever the task is, imagine an easy version of it first, gradually making it more difficult with each imagining, but keeping it equally as positive.

Exercises to aid the development of Creativity

Exercise 9.4: Interpreting Ideas

Your brain is unlikely to serve up your creative idea as a fully fledged story or template for innovation. It is likely that it will begin with fragments or simple images and the better you are at interpreting these, the more likely it is that it will grow up to be something wonderful.

It's easy to practise interpreting pictures or ideas.

1 Take a picture you like or perhaps one that you have in your house. It doesn't have to be a masterpiece, something painted by your four-year-old will work just as well.

   Give yourself two minutes to interpret it, writing down as many ideas as you can. Try to ask yourself the question 'What could it mean?'

2 Now do the same with the first verse of any poem.

Exercise 9.5: The Stimulus of Memory

This exercise develops awareness and builds your recall skills.

At the end of the day, choose three moments that have happened.

1 Spend one minute on each, writing down as much detail as you can. If it was yourself and a friend, what were you both wearing? Was there music playing? How well did your friend look today?

    Once you get used to doing this, you start to notice things in more detail, to see the world around you just a little more vividly.

2 Now take one of the three moments and play it differently. It's great if you can get something abstract or unexpected to happen. While you and a colleague were standing by the boardroom door, an opera ensemble entered or a text came from HRH asking you to the next Buckingham Palace Garden Party (unless, of course, this happens to you on a standard day!). Try to encourage your mind to create something positive and uplifting.

Exercise 9.6: Imagine the Back Story

Choose a TV drama or short story that you know reasonably well and, from this, pick one character. Now spend 10 minutes imagining the backstory of this character – what happened to them before the story begins.

▶ What are the most important experiences of their life, perhaps the crossroads or turning points?

▶ Who were the people that were most important in their life and how did they influence them?

▶ What is the character's emotional state and their experiences and aspirations at the time the story begins?

After 10 minutes, write down what you have imagined. This can take the form of simple bullet points or you can write it as a full-blown story, a prequel, if you like.

You never know, some very popular novels have started life as fan fiction!

Questions and Answers

▶ **Are there ways to make my boring job more creative?**

You can build stories into just about everything, so, at least you can keep yourself entertained while developing your creativity. Imagine the backstory of the new manager, what the house of your colleague might look like, the hideous journey to work that the accountant must have had to arrive in such a bad mood! What would the photocopier sound like if it suddenly developed a voice?

In addition to this, it's rare that there isn't some scope for making the job itself more creative. Concentrate on ways to build in ideas and collaboration. In every aspect of the work try to make changes and to think outside the box.

Organisations run on systems and, whille necessary for smooth running, it does often mean that things tend to be done the way they've been done for a good long while. Depending on your role, see if you can think of new ways to do tasks or activities, or ways that you can get members of the same organisation to work together. Perhaps choose a company charity for which employees come together to raise funds for, or begin a newsletter or suggestions box, a Friday 'moment of the week' lunch or 'creative Monday' where people get (little) prizes for ideas.

▶ **Is it bad when I use my imagination to replay what's already been?**

No, not at all. To remember positive events is constructive on all sorts of levels. It will make you feel happy and it will help to keep the memories fresh. Such memories become a very important resource for many in later life. When you remember in this way, take the time to recount the details. Think about what sensory information you recall and what emotions you felt. It is, however, as we've said before, not good to move from one replay to another continually and to miss the experiences that are unfolding around you in the present, so keep a balance.

If it's a negative memory or perhaps a good memory that causes pain due to loss, give a little time to the recall if you feel it's needed. Sit with the emotion that arrives but don't let yourself then move into a spiral of negative thoughts that may be connected to the person or event. Perhaps allow yourself say 15 minutes and then begin something else. Engage in an activity you enjoy or use one of the Mind Fitness exercises in the book to clear and reset.

Conclusion and how to build creativity into your daily life

Making full use of your imagination will help you to gain and retain 'positivity', to adapt to change and to the inevitable difficulties that crop up along the way, and to successfully employ the ABC Model to change your unhelpful beliefs. It will also enable you to be a more compassionate, empathic and fulfilled human being. Think of it this way – our thoughts are what keeps us 'entertained' for a great deal of the day.

By improving the imaginative quality of those thoughts, you will be a lot better entertained, leading to an increased interest, curiosity and engagement with everything that makes up your daily life.

Employing your imagination through the day might look like this:

- ▶ Building a short visualisation or creative exercise into your morning practise.
- ▶ Using imagination and creativity in your approach to tasks and problems.
- ▶ Making a creative activity part of your day. If this is passive, say watching a TV show rather than taking part in a local theatre group, then make sure that you have a creative response to the show.

In the six-week follow-up programme creative exercises are part of the weekend activities, but do filter them into your weekday routine if you can. What might this creative approach to life look like?

Well, first of all, play at every opportunity. If you have a child, excellent, if not, find a game you enjoy and do it whenever you can. There is nothing better than play for in-the-moment creativity.

Think about how you can adapt the things you already enjoy and spend time on. If you spend a fair amount of time, for example, posting on social media, learn how to make your photos into mini videos that you can creatively edit. Your friends will love them.

Build social activity into your day, see friends or join a group of people who share an interest. When you are reacting with and to others, employ empathy to walk in their shoes. Imagination is a key component to a healthy relationship, increasing levels of understanding and helping to keep it fresh and adaptive.

Say yes to new things and new adventures, however big or small. When someone asks if you like Lebanese food, imagine yourself liking Lebanese food. If you've never tried it and are imagining Turkish, it doesn't matter at all! You're more likely to say yes and go along.

As you go through the day, take the time to imagine. Imagine the problem solved before you begin the task. Imagine the dispute settled before you go into the meeting. If you have to make an important decision, spend a while imagining the consequences of both paths going forward, but, once the decision is made, leave the other path alone.

By responding mindfully and creatively, you will have an enhanced sense of the beauty of the world around you and the positive potential of situations. Responding creatively is an important part of the journey towards the you that will embrace change and challenges.

If you are having a difficult day, use your imagination to help you to appreciate what you have. Bring to mind the person or people to whom you are most grateful, perhaps a relative or mentor. Spend a while imagining them and the kindnesses they gave.

Very soon, employing your imagination becomes an instinctive response, the most travelled pathway, and you really do see the world with new eyes, feel more alive. We are all creative beings and harnessing that creativity is one of the most exciting parts of the process of unlocking the most vital and vibrant you.

10

Stress less

How to distinguish good stress from bad stress – and not let the stress demons take over

The term 'stress' was coined by Dr Hans Selye in the 1930s.[1] Think for a moment about what 'stress' means to you and how you would define it. A simple definition might be that it is a state of mental tension or emotional strain that results from a difficult or demanding situation.

We're going to start this chapter with a very quick exercise to give ourselves a baseline of understanding. It's a word that most of us use, but often in quite different ways.

Exercise 10.1: Interpreting Stress

A few questions for you to think about and jot down the answers in your notebook.

1   At this very moment, how would you rate your stress on a scale of 1–10?

2   When do you think you were at your most stressed in your life and why?

3   When do you think you were at your least stressed and why?

4   Of your friends, who would you say is most stressed and why?

5   Of your friends, who would you say is least stressed and why?

6   In addition, write down why you think they are stressed and how it seems to affect them

Stress can be good

Before we look in more detail at the stress response that we touched on earlier, we're going to make a bold and rather wonderful statement: *stress can be good.*

It's a statement that usually draws a reaction of surprise when we are teaching the course and, yet, we, all of us, know it to be true. You can probably think of a whole host of times in your life, from giving a presentation to delivering your child, where pressure or stress was exactly what you needed to be up to the task. An actor knows that they need nerves, the adrenaline, to be able to perform at their best; and so it is with all of us. Stress is a vital part of the way that humans function. We need a degree of stress to propel us, to make us strive and compete. And we need stress to protect us from danger.

The Buzz or Burden Continuum[2]

Realising that the goal is not to eliminate stress altogether is actually very freeing, because we all know just how difficult that would be. More than that, we secretly (or not so secretly) quite like the tingly feeling when our heart is racing just a little fast and something exciting is about to begin! At least, we like it when we believe that we are in control. When we believe we are able to do the presentation, the performance, the interview, whatever it is that has engendered the butterflies. If the task seems impossible, then it's likely that little or none of the buzz, the good feeling, will be present.

This makes sense when we look at the definition of stress by the leading authority on the subject, Professor Stephen Palmer:[3] 'Stress occurs when perceived pressure exceeds our perceived ability to cope'. The word *perceived* is, of course, key. So let's look at what happens when we believe we 'can', or at least sense that we could. What is this good stress that is not rendering us incapable and is, in fact, likely to be lending us a hand?

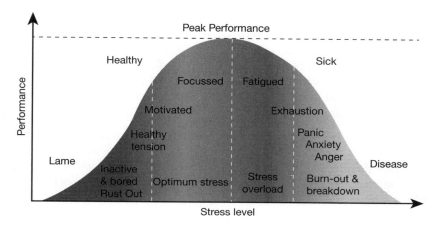

The Buzz/Burden Bell Curve

The line across the bottom of the graph above represents levels of stress against the vertical line, which measures performance.

The graph shows that there is an optimum place, that of Peak Performance, where the level of pressure (or stress) is helping us to achieve, to do and be the best that we can. This can be related to a task or situation that has taken us outside of our comfort zone but cannot be something that we perceive to be utterly unachievable. There are few things in life more stressful than being asked (by ourselves or others) to do the impossible. We know this from the goals section in which we emphasised the need to set goals that are attainable.

At the bottom left of the graph, we have an area called Rust-Out, and this can be almost as damaging to mental wellbeing as chronic stress. It is a place where nothing challenges or excites us, where we feel devoid of purpose and lose sense of our meaning. A place where nothing we are spending our time on makes the boat go any faster. A lengthy period of time in Rust-Out can lead to serious issues of low self-worth and, eventually, to depression, with one of the physical effects being a decreasingly effective immune system.

Further up the vertical line, we start to get a healthy tension. We are challenged, we are learning, we are engaged. Our motivation kicks in and we feel curious again, more alive. Our focus revives and we start to have ideas, moments of creative insight. We're more attentive to ourselves and others and more able to see the big picture. We are healthy.

At Peak Performance, at the top of the graph, we feel as though we can do anything. This is the person, perhaps, that we know we could be. This is the best self that you know is there, waiting to be unlocked. Take a moment to recall the last time you were there at Peak Performance. How did it feel? What were the steps that had taken you there? If you don't feel that you have ever been on the line, think about the closest that you have come, one side of the line or the other.

Throughout the book, there are numerous states of mind and emotion that you have been asked to identify, to marker. None is more important than this line – the place of Peak Performance. Snapshot it now. It's far too easy to be oblivious to this line approaching and to cross it unawares into the side of fatigue and ill-health.

In the West, we have never had so many people working and living on the wrong side of this line. Now see if you can remember a time where you crossed this line. Were you aware of it at the time? Often, as we've said, we are not. In many cases, we don't stop because, after all, it's just a little more of the same, so what's the problem? Or it's boiling frog syndrome and we inch there so slowly that we never even recognise that it got too hot for us to get out. Sometimes, we will have sensed the line, been warned about it even, but crossed anyway, perhaps from a fear of losing credibility or reputation or fear of recrimination from an overly demanding boss. For others your life may have a number of key ingredients and it's the mix rather than one identifiable demand that pushed you over the edge. It may be that you have been hovering close by for a while then one additional pressure has pushed you over the line.

Now see if you can think of a time when a friend or colleague crossed the line. What changed in their behaviour and emotional state once they had started down the negative slope on the right-hand side of the graph?

The good news is that there's plenty we can do to manage stress, to make sure that it's good stress and not bad stress, and that it's working for us not against us.

The stress that damages us

We mentioned the amygdala back in the Introduction to this book. If you were to take knitting needles and go through your eyes and ears (not one of our practical exercises!), on each side where these intersected would be the amygdala. As we mentioned, the amygdala has two important jobs.

Most of the time, it passes on sensory information to the prefrontal cortex, but, in times of threat or perceived threat, it instigates the fight or flight response that we have mentioned several times in the book. The diagram below shows why this is so detrimental to our health and performance. Once this is instigated, the amygdala no longer passes on the information and, the more the stress response is instigated, the harder it is to 'switch off'.

Fight, Flight versus Conscious Response?

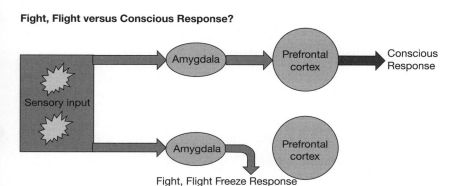

Chronic stress is an ever-present reality of life for many and is a recognised catalyst for depression, anxiety and overall poor mental and physical health. This is why, unsurprisingly, stress has a generally poor reputation and tends to be widely regarded as solely negative.

Modern life in the developed world affords many of us a higher living standard and better lifestyle opportunities than previous generations experienced. But, as our expectations have increased, so too have life's pressures – the perfect home that we aspire to live in, the regular overseas holidays, the image of ourselves that we feel we must project. Many, in addition, are juggling financial difficulties with the fast pace of our lives. There is an irony in that, while previous generations had to deal with life-threatening demands such as fighting wars and living through harsh austerity, they experienced, many would argue, far less health-damaging stress. This is due, in part, to lower lifestyle expectations than we have today, and fewer demands around living up to an ideal.

The solution starts with awareness. We need to be able to recognise the symptoms of protracted chronic stress compared to a short-lived stressful event which, when it has passed, will return us to our expected steady state.

A deer drinks at a waterhole. A lion arrives and the deer's fight or flight kicks in. It gives the deer enough adrenalin to miraculously escape the lion.

The deer goes back to feeding, her adrenalin level almost immediately back to normal. In the animal kingdom, that is what happens. In our world, it is not, because it is not clear and present danger that is the key factor, but our perceived estimation of danger or stress, the perception that we cannot cope.

We go to the meeting, come out alive, grab our waterhole drink from the coffee dispenser and our adrenalin stays high. What if the director didn't really like the report? And what about the eight things we haven't done while we were writing it? And then we remember we were stressed at breakfast this morning and snapped at the kids.

Stress easily becomes a constant, controlling and engulfing us. We begin to function less and less effectively. From there, chronic long-term stress begins to make us ill and, if left untreated, can even kill us. It's that serious. So, it's clearly something that we need to understand better and deal with when it begins to create problems for us.

As we said back in the Introduction, the stress response, a primal yet highly important human reflex, has contributed to keeping us safe through evolution. Even in our modern, less predatory world, there are real dangers. Bad things can happen, at which point our involuntary stress response helps to protect us. If we step out in the road and suddenly see a cyclist hurtling towards us, we automatically leap out of the way. It may take us a little time to recover from the shock, for the adrenaline to dissipate, but recover we will and very soon are able to go about our day none the worse for the experience.

But the modern threat is our perceived danger. It is this that is causing us long-term harm. We unwittingly create a state where our stress response is activated frequently or even continually. We create our threats from the worries that sit with us and from the unhelpful thoughts that we generate. We create them by predicting unfavourable outcomes to situations, playing out scenes in our minds that are negative and fatalistic. What if I lose my job? What if I can't get another? What if we run out of money and lose the house? What if there is a war? What will the recession do to my family? How will I survive in retirement? This kind of worry, focusing solely on imagined negative aspects of our lives, is familiar to most of us.

We wake in the night, worrying about future threats and seemingly insurmountable challenges. This pattern rapidly becomes a habitual state of worry and is manifested as chronic stress.

Stress-based illness is the main cause of working days lost in the UK and many other developed countries.

How chronic stress makes us ill

This habitual state of worry, causing our involuntary Fight or Flight Response to be constantly active, results in stress becoming our new norm. We forget what it feels like to not worry and stress. It becomes who we are. The ever-present state of worry triggers overwhelming feelings of anxiety that can quickly spiral into depression. Think of the phrase 'I was sick with worry'. Instead of a state of ease, we 'rest' in a state of unease that quickly becomes dis-ease, mental ill-health.

When we perceive danger, stress hormones (including adrenalin and cortisol) are released by the brain to prepare our body to deal with the impending threat. These make their way along blood vessels, reaching the heart. Adrenalin causes the heart to beat faster and raises blood pressure so that we're ready to face the exertion required to deal with the threat. Cortisol, when constantly released into the arteries, contributes to the build-up of cholesterol, gradually blocking the arteries and raising the risk of a heart attack or a stroke.

At this point, there's much more happening to us. When your brain senses stress, it activates the autonomic nervous system and, in turn, stress signals are transmitted to the intestinal nervous system. As we said in Chapter 8, that's when you feel butterflies in your stomach or the churning sensation so linked to dread or worry.

That gut activity starts to alter the contractions that help food to pass through the digestive system, thereby making you more susceptible to irritable bowel syndrome. When the gut becomes sensitive you're also more likely to experience heartburn or acid reflux. This process can also change the composition and function of gut bacteria. Scientists are now linking these bacterial changes to depression and it has long been known that digestive imbalance issues can lead to a wide range of overall health problems.

And the list goes on. Chronic stress can lead to weight gain, especially through an increase in waistline fat. This is because cortisol increases your appetite, making you crave comfort foods that tend to be energy-dense, high-carbohydrate type junk foods. The brain is preparing us to physically fight the expected danger and is helping us to increase our energy reserves. It's a pretty impressive process; we're being prepared to fight or flee. It's a shame that if we don't need that physical accelerator at this time we simply store the fat.

This waistline fat, known also as deep belly fat, increases the chances of us developing heart disease and becoming insulin resistant, which leads to diabetes. Chronic stress dampens the function of immune cells, making us more susceptible to infections and also slows down the rate of healing. This explains why workers take time off sick with genuine physical illness that doesn't properly reflect the stress-based nature of their incapacity. For this reason, the official figures for stress-based working days lost may be drastically understated. People may simply be unaware that their poor health comes as a result of stress, anxiety or depression.

Chronic stress also contributes to premature ageing and is known to be a trigger for skin complaints, headaches, hair loss, lack of sex drive, impotency, muscle pain, poor concentration and fatigue. We can only imagine the additional pressure that such symptoms generate for people already suffering stress.

How to keep the stress demons at bay

The first thing to remember is that, if you consider yourself a worrier, even a 'born worrier', you are likely to have practised this so often that you will have become a master at it. It has become your reflex action, your route of least resistance. Now is the time to practise 'not worrying!' As you feel the tension start to set in, pick one of the mindfulness exercises from earlier in the book or one of the exercises at the end of this chapter. It's useful to make one of them your go-to stress buster exercise. That will become your new habit and you'll be able to gain the desired sense of calm more quickly.

And, if it seems hard at first, remember that Neuroplasticity tells us that the deepest possible change can be achieved. It is new science based on old philosophy – ancient Buddhist texts speak of the 'accommodating capacity of the mind', which they call 'malleability'.

Getting to the root of the stress

▶ **Work on your Unhelpful Beliefs.** It is most important to use the ABC Model to identify the Unhelpful Beliefs that are at the root of the stress. Because of the negative spiral in which the ANTs operate, it is likely that you have constructed five or six problems that you have attached to the real issue. There is sometimes an overwhelming sense of release as people on our courses identify the root cause that has been tying them in knots.

▶ **Build yourself a strong Self-Image.** Self-doubt is an exhausting and corrosive process. Make sure that your new Self-Image is authentic. Some of the most stressed and miserable people are those struggling to be something that they are not.

▶ **Practise acceptance.** It is worth remembering that, even if you have managed to swap all your rigid demands to preferences, there will be times when those preferences will not be met and you will need to practise acceptance and move on.

▶ **Remember to combat moments of stress by countering them with a moment of evidenced success.** Say it out loud if you are somewhere that you can. You might say, 'I know I am facing difficulties with the bid that I am currently writing, but last year I got a bid accepted for twice as much money.' The two don't even need to be related – it could be, 'But last night I won a prize for my karaoke version of Monster Mash!' I (BW) always start with a loud 'aha' in pirate (panto) style because it puts me in the right mood to break the negative feeling. If you catch a worry or ANT, pounce on it and swap with a success. 'Aha! I might be worrying about the hideous noises coming from the boiler, but yesterday I handed my editor a chapter of this book/taught my daughter her first nursery rhyme/cooked the best bread pudding in the history of cakes!'

▶ **Give yourself recovery time and relaxation.** As we have said, we all need downtime. In our modern world of multifaceted environments, with the fast flow of information and social media keeping us constantly alert, this has never been more true. Relaxation is hugely important. One helpful technique is to try to build just a few moments of relaxation into the most stressful of activities, the most stressful of days. For example, while doing a task on your tablet/iPad, find three times to stand and walk three paces, focussing on the soles of your feet. Or set your alarm to go off four times through the busiest days; when it sounds, do a 30-second relaxation, real or imagined. A good one is releasing your leg muscles and bottom muscles as you sit and feel them contact with the chair, or simply have a really good stretch. You would imagine that such minuscule moments of relaxation couldn't possibly have an effect, but try them. You might be surprised.

▶ **Hit the clear button in moments of transition.** Do this so that you don't carry tension or worry from one task or area of your life to the next.

▶ **Stop multitasking.** One of the worst examples of conventional wisdom of the modern age was the acceptance of multitasking as a good thing. Give it up if you haven't already! I (BW) was renowned for my multitasking skills. Giving them up was almost as hard as getting rid of an addiction! It's also one of the best things I ever did. Focussing on one thing, in the present, goes a very long way to reducing stress.

▶ **Don't get phased by decisions.** Take your time to weigh up the options and potential consequences, and then choose. Remember that getting into the habit of making little decisions often and quickly will enable you to make important decisions more easily.

▶ **Don't try too hard.** Remember that the state that you are aiming for is relaxed but alert. You can certainly cause stress by trying too hard to be focussed and particularly by concentrating on the outcome rather than the process. Both surgeons and golfers talk about 'purpose trauma' that can suddenly make it impossible to keep your hand still as you take up the scalpel or club. Many of us have experienced the same trauma when we have tried to thread a needle or pour water into a bottle. If this happens to you, forget the outcome and bring your attention back to the present, the sensations of the doing.

How to keep the buzz and the flow

A few quick techniques to keep you engaged and motivated and in the right part of the Buzz Burden Chart.

▶ Look at things and say to yourself, 'I find that absolutely fascinating because …' Most of the time, your subconscious will take over and give you a reason! Remember, it is our interest in anything that makes it seem extraordinary.

▶ If you need to be interested in something that you don't find fascinating (for example your job or the company you're working for), imagine that you own the company or invented the product that it is centred around – whatever gives you the feeling of having a vested interest.

▶ If you need to be interested in a person you find less than fascinating, seek out one point of identification, one thing that you have in common. It is a technique used by actors when they have to play characters they don't feel particularly drawn to.

▶ Keep engaged with others and the external world. If you've gone through a period of stress, you may find that one of the results is that you have isolated yourself. Take small steps to join back into the world of connected living.

▶ Be inspired! Keep a notebook of inspiring quotes and facts about inspiring people!

▶ Eat a frog for breakfast. This is a time-management technique that we really love. If you have something to do that you're dreading, do it first. Otherwise, our cantankerous brain will use up a great deal of time worrying about it and will probably let in the ANTs.

▶ Be creative! Try to do at least one creative thing a day. Buy a mindfulness colouring book, write a poem, rearrange an area of your house to make it look beautiful. Do one of the creative exercises in Chapter 9.

▶ Note down five things you'd like to do but haven't done. Next to each, write the reason that you haven't done it. Next to the reason, write a counter argument – an argument that you would give to a friend if you were persuading them that they should.

Practise mindfulness

Our last and most important tip for increasing your motivation would also be our most important tip for reducing stress – practising mindfulness. Mindfulness places you in the most exciting time because now is the only thing that is ever happening. Everything that seemed ordinary and even tedious becomes special and fascinating, if you really focus on it. A trivial conversation is only trivial if it is purposeless, devoid of meaning. It takes on a whole new dimension if you are genuinely fascinated by a shopping trip or a friend's new bag. We work a lot with people with disabilities and, for many, the only time and place they can inhabit is the moment. If you have a conversation about their new watch or the flavour of the cake, it is everything to them, and that is both humbling and refreshing. Sylvia Borstein, in her excellent book *Don't Just Do Something, Sit There*, describes mindfulness as awakening to the happiness of the uncomplicated moment![4] I think this captures it perfectly. It gives you the ability to have a healing perspective on life: positive, compassionate and accepting.

Much of Chapter 6, Think your Best Think, is about freeing yourself from limited vision, from cognitive bias. Mindfulness, because it returns you to a state of centred neutrality, really helps with this.

For me (BW) mindfulness brings together both sides of the stress/motivation Buzz/Burden line. It gives you increased ability to be focussed, in flow and energised while, at the same time, engendering a fundamental response that is calm. Think about the line of optimum performance, it will always be in the now.

Three mindfulness exercises

Many people have to get past the pressing idea that they don't have time to just sit there for 10 minutes. You are likely to gain back, as we've said, much more than your 10 minutes if the rest of the day contains considerably more focussed thought than it would otherwise have done. But, essentially, it's about intention and weight of purpose. It is you deciding that, in order to implement change in your life so that you can be happier and healthier and achieve the things that are important to you, it is worth 10 minutes. It's a tiny slot in a 24-hour day and, really, what could be more important?

Two of the following exercises are done while sitting and one while walking. Only the Body Scan in Chapter 8 needs to be done lying down. This is because it is not about being so relaxed that you fall asleep; it is getting yourself to a state where you are alert as well as relaxed. When I (BW) am sitting, I think of my spine being held, but the muscles around it being relaxed. It is certainly possible to successfully practise mindfulness lying down or, indeed, standing on your head, but either would be considerably more difficult for a beginner.

When we practise, we can have a goal, say to be able to pay attention calmly in any given situation, but it's important, as you do each exercise, not to have an agenda, not even one of keeping your focus in the place described in the exercise. If you don't keep your focus, just gently bring it back.

Finally, before you begin any exercise, take a moment to prepare. Preparing is something we don't give as much attention to as we should. It's not a coincidence that so many activities that require focus are preceded by 'ready, steady, go' or 'take aim, fire'. It will transition you in and help you to look forward to the exercise. It's the glorious pleasure of unpacking that begins a holiday, preparing you for adventure. To prepare I (BW) just clear a bit of space around me and look at three gifts that my daughter has brought me over the years for a second or two each. I have a friend who wafts around lavender room spray!

Exercise 10.2: Mindful Walking

You can, of course, walk mindfully around your home. If you need to do this, corridors are good, but we strongly suggest that you walk outside. Science has now proved a benefit to the brain that lasts for several hours from walking in a natural environment.[5] As with so many pieces of research currently coming in, it's not a surprise.

So choose a place where you feel inspired and welcome, somewhere you like.

▶ **Part one.** For the first minute, concentrate only on you, on the movement of your body as you step. Start by honing in on the weight as it moves through your feet and work your way upwards, noticing how each part of your body is connected and responds to the movement. Notice whether or not the rhythm of your breath corresponds to the rhythm of your steps.

▶ **Part two.** For eight minutes, simply notice the wonderful thing that is nature around you. Let your attention be drawn to the smallest mark on the tree or the wildest shape of a cloud on the horizon. Notice the sounds, the smells and the temperature of the air against your skin. Notice the light and shade around you and any signs of life. As you practise, imagine that you are seeing this piece of bark, this magpie, this sunflower for the very first time. You are; you may have seen a sunflower, but never this one, in this light, on this day. Make no assumptions. Imagine you are an alien just landed on Earth and seeing everything afresh. The idea is not simply to see everything but to see it with new eyes. As you notice, perhaps for the first time since you were a child, the structure of the sunflower, glory in it – yes it's not too strong a word. The release of gratitude is extraordinary.

▶ **Part three.** For the last minute, just do parts one and two at the same time. Hold in your consciousness, your awareness of you, your body, your breath, your movement and also take in the awareness of the natural world in which you are walking. It's the most wonderful way to gain or regain a sense of connection.

Exercise 10.3: Mindful Eating

For the first time, indulge yourself by trying mindful eating with a chocolate. If you don't like chocolate, a strawberry is good.

Begin by placing the chocolate on your hand. Spend a minute noticing the shape, the texture, the weight.

Bring the chocolate up to your face and spend a while only using smell. Notice anything, everything. Know, from the smell, how you expect the chocolate to taste.

Notice any changes in your body. Are you beginning to salivate? What exactly does that feel like? Are you feeling excited? This is likely as the dopamine is released. Perhaps you have a pang of hunger or the tension of appetite. What does this feel like?

Now place the chocolate on your tongue, but do not bite it. Notice the texture and the taste and, again, any physical responses in your mouth or any part of your body. What words would you use to describe the sensations?

And, finally, eat the sweet, but eat it slowly and bring every sense to the experience. How does the taste feel in different parts of your mouth? How does the swallowing reflex work? Which is the most exquisite moment?

It is likely that you will have experienced the sensation of taste more intensely than usual, perhaps more intensely than you ever have. Sometimes, we get this when we are abroad or away from common experience and try something with heightened anticipation, a custard in Lisbon, a truffle in France. It is the equivalent of walking with new eyes.

Of course, it's good to eat every meal with an awareness that is mindful, to give your full focus to the eating. The gratitude aroused by the saying of grace before meals in the past used to set up this experience. Think about how much more you have tasted, experienced the food when a friend has gone to a lot of trouble cooking it for you or when your child presents you with something they have prepared for the first time.

Exercise 10.4: Mindful Breathing

We've done Image Breathing, which is probably our favourite exercise, a few times, but we'll do one here that simply focusses on the breath.

First, sit in a comfortable position, perhaps with your hands on your knees and your feet flat on the floor. Notice any physical sensations for a few moments and then take your attention to your breath.

Don't search for the sensation of your breath, just be aware of it when it arrives for you. An important distinction is waiting rather than scanning. As it does so, be aware of the now. People experience the breath in a number of different ways.

Be as precise as you can in your noticing. You may notice it as the changing movement of your stomach. You may notice it as pressure or tension in the rib cage or chest. You may notice it as a tingling sensation in your nose.

Some people notice the breath move down the spine or even feel it through the whole body. There is no right or wrong, it is simply a deepening of awareness.

Once you have relaxed into this noticing, it is likely that you will notice the small gaps between breaths and even the tiny gap between the in-breath and the out-breath. Focus on these for the last minute of the exercise.

After the exercise, just know what these gaps, these moments of transitions felt like. This is why, in this exercise, we are concentrating only on the breath. I (BW) found that once I was familiar with this I was more able to see/feel gaps and employ them in many situations. If someone was angry, I more easily felt a moment of reflective space in which I could rest before giving a more measured, conditioned response. Being able to rest in the moment of transition, between the waves on the beach, between leaving your car and entering your home space, also seems to bring a sense of slowing, of calming, of being given more time.

Questions and Answers

▶ **How can I prepare for what I know will be a stressful day?**

It's really important to give yourself a few minutes before you begin, to get yourself into the best possible place. Do an exercise or two before you leave the house or when you get to your place of work.

But it's really about awareness. If you know what the likely stresses will be, you can prepare. If you expect that a demanding boss will shout, your preparation will go a long way to preventing you from taking it personally. Check in with yourself, perhaps on the hour every hour, simply asking, how am I now? Doing OK! Good. Carry on! If you need to, do a quick exercise, perhaps Foxhole in My Mind (see page 24), which is excellent for reducing stress.

▶ **If I don't worry about things, doesn't it mean I don't care about them?**

First, check whether your concern is that you will actually stop caring or whether it is *seeming* not to care that is the concern. If it's the former, then no, worry and care are not bound together or even close cousins. In fact, we worry about many things that we don't care about at all. If you care about something, you want to be in the best emotional and mental state to act upon your care, so ditch the worry and have more time and space for passion.

Conclusion

Everything we have covered in the book will help you to be less stressed and more motivated and engaged. You know how to reposition an event or situation if you're Awfulising. You know how to course-correct, and that is essential. Today is just today. When coaching, we sometimes ask how important an event will seem when looking back on it in two years from now, or five.

You know how to stay positive and curious, to expect that deep investigation will always reveal more. Remember that being able to cope with stress does not mean sailing along on a still, never changing sea. It is being able to return to a state of balance while retaining creative passion. There will be highs and there will be lows. The lows you know to sit with, learn from and move on. And having finally let go of the fear that if you give yourself fully to the highs you will only mourn their eventual passing, you will come to enjoy each and every positive experience with a hopeful and open heart.

11

Coping with bad stuff

How to deal with negative emotions and gradually change them

Imagine a world without emotions. It would be like living in a two-dimensional existence and it would certainly be almost impossible, without care and passion, to have purpose and meaning.

While Mind Fitness will enable you to manage your negative emotions and gradually replace some of them with feelings that are unlikely to disturb and sabotage you, it is in no way a process of losing your emotions.

Even the negative emotions are an important part of life. If we lose someone through either a break up or bereavement, it is right, and in fact vital, that we feel sad. The key is learning to sit with the sadness and not let it lead you into the downward spiral. I (BW) think of keeping the sadness for myself rather than handing it over to the ANTs. It also means that the deep sadness is felt when there is a reason for it; we would not slip into it if we lost a favourite bag. We all have enough 'big stuff' in our lives to deal with. Learning not to 'sweat the small stuff' is an incredibly useful tool.

We sometimes find that people we work with have cut off their emotional response. Often they have built a wall to protect themselves but, of course, it is keeping out all that is good as well as all that is bad. This may be a valid temporary response to real trauma but even then we must find a way to switch the emotions back on. If it continues, we create negative beliefs to sustain and reinforce it, essentially prolonging the trauma. But with a combination of reframing these beliefs, accepting where we are and sitting with the emotion, we can start to move on. The re-entry to the world of emotions has been likened to the feeling of 'waking up.'

What is an Emotion?

An emotion is a conscious experience characterised by mental activity and a certain degree of pleasure or displeasure.

Emotions are certainly the driving force behind many of our behaviours, both helpful and unhelpful. Our brain, as you know, is hard wired to look out for threats or rewards. When it sees them, it releases chemicals that travel from our brain and through our body. The emotions we feel are the effect of these chemical messages.

An emotional reaction has many parts:

▶ Our brain changes what is happening in our body. For example, our heart will beat faster if we're angry or scared, we'll get tears in our eyes when we are sad and our voice will change.

▶ Our brain starts working differently as we 'look' to reinforce the emotion – if we're scared, we will see danger in almost any situation and, if we're happy, we'll start to notice things we like.

▶ Our behaviour will change – we may fight if we're angry, run away if we are scared and hide ourselves away if we are sad.

The 'feeling' kicks in subconsciously and our emotions can hijack our brain, making it very difficult to think rationally. Emotions are incredibly important to almost all of us. The pursuit of happiness has been the grail for many cultures ancient and modern. You are probably reading this book because you want to feel happy more of the time and bad less of the time.

Why are Emotions important?

On the most basic level, emotions are important because they mean that you can enjoy life – love your partner and children, appreciate the things you have and the glorious natural world, relish a contentment in old age and feel a sense of achievement and joy when you do something great or help another person.

They are also incredibly important to the whole Mind Fitness process of change. Our emotions are beacons or markers; if we feel a sense of unease or disquiet or even sadness or fear, it sounds an alarm and we know that we have let in the ANTs. It's time to focus and calm the noise. We are also able to make changes more quickly and more effectively if our rational thought is accompanied by a deep desire or passion to change. The more that we can invest emotionally, the more vigour we can bring to the change, the more likely the process will be effective. In fact, building new neural pathways is as much about intensity as repetition; if you love going for a run now that you are not smoking, that will help to establish the new behaviour more quickly.

Positive emotions also create the environment that gives birth to insightful thoughts and ideas. It's not enough to dispel the negative, we need also to bring in the positive. We must allow ourselves to be enthusiastic, curious and thrilled and, if we find ourselves short of these resources, we must commit to nurturing them. It can be done.

Exercise 11.1: Curiosity

This exercise is about using curiosity to fuel a positive perception of the world. Simply write down 10 'I wonders'. They can be about anything that interests you.

For example:

▶ I wonder who built the Great Sphinx of Giza and how they did it

▶ I wonder what led the Beatles to write 'Yellow Submarine'

▶ I wonder where in the world the fantastic coffee in my cupboard comes from

How many Emotions are there?

Just for fun, try to make a list before you read on. Emotions are incredibly hard to describe and define (ask any translator) and it's likely that, if you and I both described the difference between, say, love and compassion, it would not be the same. And, if you imagine an emotion when you are in a good mood or bad mood, it will probably 'feel' different. The subtleties of language are never more apparent than when describing an emotion. It is why poets and artists can make us feel something that we have never felt before. The not exclusive list of emotions we came up with is:

Range of emotions

Acceptance	Depression	Paranoia
Affection	Disappointment	Pity
Aggression	Disgust	Pleasure
Ambivalence	Doubt	Pride
Anger	Homesickness	Rage
Apathy	Hunger	Regret
Anxiety	Hurt	Remorse
Boredom	Hysteria	Shame
Compassion	Interest	Sorrow
Confusion	Jealousy	Suffering
Concern	Loneliness	Surprise
Contempt	Love	Sympathy

Exercise 11.2: Your Habitual Emotions

Using either our list or your own, circle the six emotions that you feel most often.

Of the six, pick the three that seem most different from the others.

Note by these three when you last felt them and in what circumstances. Try to describe in detail how the emotion made you feel.

Negative Emotions

As we've said, we can see our negative emotions as warning signs or alarms. They tell us that something is wrong and needs to be challenged or changed. Train yourself, if you can, to be grateful for them. Thank goodness they came along for how would you have known otherwise?

Our habitual negative emotions, particularly our fear and our anger, are states that we have adopted in response to a problem. At some point, probably way back, we moved into them because we saw them, either consciously or unconsciously, as a solution and we didn't know any other way.

Very quickly, these negative emotions 'became' us. We've woven a thousand negative thoughts around them and thrown in self-pity and resentment.

We need have no self-recrimination or remorse. It happened. Now that we understand and accept this, we can use the ABC Model to help us to adopt a new response. Enjoying a life where we are not crushed or defeated by these negative emotions is about managing them, not suppressing them. The attempt to do the latter results in harsh mood swings and very little sense of contentment.

We'll have a quick look at three of the most common negative emotions and then we'll look at the Rational Emotive Behavioural Therapy (REBT) approach to move negative harmful emotions to less harmful versions of the same emotional state.

Anxiety

The result of our mind evaluating a threat (real or perceived) is fear, producing the emotion of anxiety. Then, once we have entered the state of anxiety, it's impossible to be rational; our mind interprets everything through the lense of worry and fear. As we have said, it is future-focussed, based on fear of what might happen. As soon as we become aware of the anxiety, it's important to use an exercise to get ourselves back into a state in which we can think clearly and rationally.

Always bear in mind the wonderful quote, 'We have nothing to fear but fear itself' (Franklin D Roosevelt).[1] We all understand that bullying is when you take away someone's peace of mind by making them afraid and, yet, we do this to ourselves all the time. And there is the equally wonderful, 'Never take counsel of your fears,' by Stonewall Jackson.[2] If such thoughts come into our mind, we can choose not to listen. Imagine how little we would trust an advisor or leader who seemed to be in a constant state of terror!

Anger

In terms of cognitive bias and conditioned behaviour, remember that we learned way back to cry and scream when we needed feeding. Many of us still do this when we have a problem that needs solving.

If you are driven by anger, it is worth checking back to your Self-Image. Those who are most easily angered or offended are usually those with a weaker Self-Image or lower sense of self-value. Use the exercises in Chapter 7 to strengthen and reinforce your Self-Image.

And to avoid anger:

▶ Don't expect people to behave in the way you would, or to have your set of rules or beliefs

▶ Don't expect more of yourself than you would of other people

Hurt

Even the deepest wounds heal faster when we don't infect and re-infect ourselves with the ANTs and the negative spiral.

It may be, however, that you are holding on to the hurt. The intensity of any emotion, especially pain, can be addictive. Poets talk of the exquisiteness of pain and we can certainly get a perverse pleasure from experiencing it. If we are not careful, we can trap ourselves in a vain endeavour to prove that we are, at least, alive. And it may feel empty for a short while when the hurt, the pain, loses its sting. But, with the help of a strong Self-Image reinforced with compassion and meaning, the space can be filled with positive emotions.

Exercise 11.3: Releasing Emotions

There's a great visualisation exercise that we can do to release the negative emotions we are feeling, before we move on to look at how to reframe them.

Close your eyes and stand in an open position, feet shoulder width apart, your arms down by your sides but a few centimetres away from the sides of your body. Make sure that your spine is straight and that you feel centred.

Now imagine that your body is full of nasty emotions. We usually imagine them in the order in which they first occur to us, which often relates to the emotions that are more prevalent at the time. Some people like to imagine the emotions as liquids, gas or colours.

Once you are 'full', imagine the emotions draining down through your body and seeping into the ground. Let your muscles soften as the tension attached to the emotion drains away.

Unhealthy Negative Emotions[3] as identified by REBT

REBT doesn't try to banish negative emotions and make us strive for a false nirvana of ecstatic happiness. By learning to identify and confront troublesome emotions we can begin to reframe the way we think, behave and feel. We'll go through that process step by step, but, first, let's take a closer look at the emotions.

The positive emotions we feel, such as happiness, euphoria, affection or love, give us pleasure so they clearly aren't going to cause us issues. It's the negative emotions that cause us upset and just identifying these is hard because there are many to choose from.

REBT makes the identification process far less complicated by compressing the range of negative emotions to just eight. These are termed as Unhealthy Negative Emotions (UNEs).

Here they are along with their very specific associated themes:

Unhealthy Negative Emotion	Theme
Anxiety	Threat or danger
Depression	Significant loss, failure
Guilt	Moral lapse, hurting others
Anger	Personal rules violated, frustration
Shame	Perceived weakness or defect revealed to others
Hurt	Let down or treated badly
Envy	Covet good fortune of others
Jealousy	Threat to a relationship posed by another

When you are in a difficult situation, dealing with adversity, it can feel very challenging to pinpoint your exact emotional response. It's vitally important that we learn to do this so that we can start the process of emotional reframing. The first task is being able to recognise emotions from feelings.

Feelings versus Emotions

A feeling is an emotional experience – brief and episodic.

An emotion lies beneath these feelings, at the core. Emotions endure for years, sometimes for a lifetime, and predispose us to emotional experiences, feelings, as well as to thoughts and actions.

We sometimes have to drill down through several feelings to reach the underlying emotion. For example, if a neighbour repeatedly throws loud late-night parties, we might say that we are fed up, annoyed and hacked off before reaching the underlying emotion of anger.

Once we have identified the emotion, we are ready to make changes. The whole Mind Fitness process helps us to be more aware of our emotions so that we are better and sooner able to identify and deal with the unhealthy negative ones that trip us up.

There are other challenges, such as understanding meta emotions – the emotions we experience about our emotions! As an example, Fred may feel anger over an affair he had with a work colleague. The anger, in this case, is directed at himself for his perceived weakness that led to the shame he feels for causing upset to his family and for his uncharacteristic moral lapse.

By identifying the main emotion, in this case shame, we are able to begin reframing that emotion in order to deal with the secondary emotion, anger.

Exercise 11.4: Identifying Emotions

At a specific time (say after a show or meal), ask a friend to tell you the emotions they are feeling.

Focus in on any that are negative. See if you can gradually unpick them and pull them back to one of the eight identified emotions. If necessary, keep asking the question 'and how does that make you feel?'.

Healthy Negative Emotions

Using the REBT model, the alternative to UNEs are Healthy Negative Emotions (HNEs.)

The term Healthy Negative Emotions may feel a little odd at first. How could negative emotions ever be regarded as healthy? But they can.

This table shows the UNE and corresponding HNE.

Unhealthy Negative Emotion (UNE)	Healthy Negative Emotion (HNE)
Anxiety	Concern
Depression	Sadness
Guilt	Remorse
Anger	Healthy anger
Shame	Disappointment
Hurt	Sorrow
Jealousy	Healthy jealousy
Envy	Healthy envy

At first glance, healthy anger could feel like a misnomer. How could any anger be regarded as healthy? Or jealousy? It doesn't immediately make sense. We've already seen the themes associated with the UNEs. Let's take a look at each emotional reframing and associated changes in behaviour.

Anxiety to Concern

Anxiety is future-focussed. It triggers our Stress Response. It causes worry and unhappiness. We may find that we're less prepared to confront adversity when we feel anxious.

Concern allows us to acknowledge that there is a problem, develop understanding that then means we can begin to confront the issues and develop a rationally considered, coherent plan to respond.

Depression to Sadness

Depression is past-focussed. It can cause people to withdraw and disengage from society. The ABC Model by changing rigid demand-based beliefs into healthier preferences, allows us to reduce the extreme symptoms of depression into sadness.

Sadness It's OK to feel sad. We can sit with the sadness, acknowledge that we are sad about a situation, but we will be able to engage and connect. The emotion of sadness is about acceptance encouraging self-compassion, states that help us to heal.

Guilt to Remorse

Guilt is aligned closely with damning or self-criticism. One unfortunate action is the thing that we now feel universally defines us as a bad person: 'I'm no good. I did a bad thing and that makes me a bad person.'

Remorse acknowledges the bad act or deed but doesn't let it define us: 'I did a bad thing and I am remorseful for that, but it doesn't mean that bad thing defines me as a bad person.'

Anger to Healthy Anger

Anger (rage) can be blind. Nothing was ever solved in anger. Things are said and done that are later regretted, and revenge is planned and acted out. Anger diminishes our powers of emotional control, causing us to disturb ourselves in the extreme. Aggression and anger go hand in hand.

Healthy Anger (annoyance) acknowledges injustice or wrongdoing, but the reaction is calm though assertive behaviour. Assertion is vastly preferential to aggression. We keep control and can therefore respond to the situation in a firm but measured way. This is a key component of high Emotional Intelligence.

Shame to Disappointment

Shame is experienced when we feel personal exposure. We have been found out. Our shameful secret has been revealed. We have been caught doing something for which we believe others will judge us unfavourably. We may choose to avoid our accusers or detractors and be unable to look them in the eye.

Disappointment allows us to reframe our feelings in a compassionate and self-accepting way. We are able to take a balanced view of the expected disapproval from others and face the situation without being compelled to hide away.

Hurt to Sorrow

Hurt arises from the perception that others have treated us badly or unfairly: 'You hurt my feelings.' Their treatment of us is unjust. When we're hurt, we're more likely to irrationally overestimate the degree of the perceived slight against us. We revisit previous misdemeanours and build a body of 'evidence'. We may sulk, wishing to punish the perpetrator with silence or a piece of our mind.

Sorrow acknowledges that an unfortunate situation with another exists, but it's viewed realistically and rationally so that it doesn't become over-thought. When we experience the less-charged state of sorrow, we can rationally face the perpetrator to calmly work towards resolving the conflict.

Jealousy to Healthy Jealousy

Jealousy is such a destructive emotion. It's driven people to misery and murder. Often confused with envy, jealousy is anxiety about a threat or perceived threat to an important relationship. Jealousy compels us to question the activities of a suspected errant loved one. We may seek assurances of love and faithfulness, look for signs of infidelity or simply sulk. Marriages break down and close friendships are destroyed due to jealousy. The jealousy may be professional rather than romantic jealousy, applying threat to a professional relationship.

Healthy Jealousy is concern about a threat to an important relationship. It is about balance and rationality. It's understanding that our partner may be physically attractive to others or may find others attractive, without wishing to act on that. Our partner may chat to someone at a party without that implying romantic or sexual intent. We give our partner space and freedom. We trust unless evidence to the contrary is overwhelming.

Envy to Healthy Envy

Envy The coveting of something that someone else has. Envy, especially social envy, has become a significant societal issue with social media giving unprecedented access to others' lives. Keeping up with the Jones's has been superseded by our need to compare ourselves to and keep up with, well, everyone. We see the holidays our 'friends' are taking, their house in Tuscany being renovated, the perfect family party pictures and that expensive new car they've just taken delivery of. How do they have all that and I don't? I want that lifestyle. The fact that I haven't means I'm a worthless failure.

Healthy Envy To be able to desire the possessions of others or their perceived lifestyle, but not to be eaten up by that desire. To allow others to have that which you would like and accept the situation comfortably. Aspire to achieve those things or acquire those possessions if that is what you truly desire, but not through avarice or the need to compete.

How to reframe UNEs to HNEs

The benefits of learning to adopt HNEs is clear. HNEs allow us to be more rational, measured and to stay calm and in control.

The whole Mind Fitness process is likely to bring latent emotions into the realm of your conscious thoughts. Many of these will be positive, which is brilliant; others will be negative, and this is where we begin to work on these.

REBT stresses that emotional problems are based on irrational thinking and that, if we are to address these problems, we need to change the thinking to its rational equivalent.

A	B	C
Adversity	Irrational Beliefs	Unhealthy Negative Emotion
Adversity	Rational Beliefs	Healthy Negative Emotion

And you already know the way that this is done – by using the ABC Model. So this is the last piece in the ABC puzzle.

Using the ABC to reframe Unhealthy Negative Emotions: example – neighbour conflict

Scenario 1 – With Demands and UNEs

A Activating Event

George was suffering another evening of noise from his new next door neighbours. He'd not met them as they'd only been there a week, but every evening, late into the night, they had played loud music. George had had enough.

B Belief

You must not encroach on my world with your loud music. It's awful that you're so unthoughtful. You're utter morons!

C Consequence

George can take no more. He marches round to next door and lets them have it. He tells them what he thinks. He'll show them. A vicious argument ensues, with insults and threats traded. The neighbour tells George to get lost (or words to that effect) and slams the door. They turn the music up louder!

Emotional – Anger, anxiety, hurt

Behavioural – Uncontrolled aggression, shouting, swearing, making threats of physical violence

Physiological (symptoms) – Pounding heart, head hurting, breathing heavily. George feels like he's about to have a heart attack.

Scenario 2 – With Preferences and Healthy Negative Emotions

A Activating Event

George was suffering another evening of noise from his new next door neighbours. He'd not met them as they'd only been there a week, but every evening, late into the night, they had played loud music. George feels that the time is right to confront the problem.

B Belief

I would prefer that we find a way to live comfortably next door to one another. Loud music from next door every evening is not acceptable.

I suspect that they're not aware of how thin the walls are rather than being malicious.

C Consequence

Emotional – Healthy Anger, Concern, Sorrow

Behavioural – George pops next door, calmly introduces himself in a friendly way and goes on to explain that the connecting walls are very thin. He smiles and asks that they keep the music levels down. The neighbour is mortified and apologises profusely. She and her partner didn't realise. George invites them over for get to know you drinks at the weekend. They accept and apologise again. The music is turned off.

Physiological (symptoms) – George feels some anticipation in the form of mild butterflies as he knocks on the door, but he's going to be assertive, not aggressive, so he feels in control and will do his best to find compromise.

Exercise 11.5: Reframing an Unhealthy Negative Emotion

Select a UNE that you feel or have recently felt.

Identify the irrational or rigid belief that is causing the emotional problem.

Follow the process used in the example above, changing the irrational to a rational belief, the UNE to its healthy equivalent.

Complete the table below:

Adversity	Irrational belief	UNE	Rational (helpful) belief	HNE

The positive emotions

As we have said, positive emotions are there for you to use in negotiating the path to a happier and more productive you. If you are working on a stronger Self-Image, then invest emotionally in this. It is not just important that you think well of yourself but that you love yourself. It sounds trite, but emotions are what makes the relationship between you and your mind dynamic. If this still feels too big a step, then love aspects of you if you can – your voice, your hands, your sense of humour until you have so many that you make a compassionate kaleidoscope of the whole you.

Exercise 11.6: Intensifying a Positive Emotion

Start by sitting down in a comfortable position with your eyes closed.

Take a moment to identify a time when you felt joy or love. Spend two minutes recalling the time or experience. As we have said, every emotion manifests itself physically so try to be as detailed as you can, as you recall.

Look at the kind of joy that made you laugh or smile or jump up and down. Try to connect the feeling with the action; if you're not certain what I mean, think about the purring of a cat or the way that a dog wags its tail.

Now allow the emotion to intensify and the action to swell or grow. If it was the dog, he may now be panting or chasing his tail around in a circle.

Once you have really invested in the experience, try to think of how you are feeling now that you are recalling it. It's a great place to return to when you need a bit of a boost or when it feels harder than usual to be grateful for the everyday things in your life.

Happiness

For us to really employ our abilities to be happy, it's vital that, as individuals and as a society, we move away from the prevailing idea that suffering is somehow good, that it is the way to the light. We even think that if we expect the best it will somehow trip us up, that we are 'tempting fate'. Or we think that if we imagine the worst then anything else will seem good in comparison. It won't! Expect the worst and it's likely that your brain will focus on this and do it's best to deliver it. Instead, expect the best, the very best that you can imagine. When we are happy, we fulfil our individual potential, as well as our potential to help others. We think better, perform better and are healthier when we are happy.

So, what is this wonderful feeling called happiness? Dr John A. Shindler[4] describes it as a 'state of mind in which our thinking is pleasant a good share of the time'. That seems good to us.

The essential thing, as you will by now have realised, is that happiness is an attitude, a mental habit. You can acquire it by:

- ▶ being in the moment
- ▶ having a positive Self-Image
- ▶ employing gratitude and compassion
- ▶ not allowing in the ANTs when you sit with a negative emotion
- ▶ moving negative, unhelpful emotions to more helpful versions of the same state
- ▶ challenging and changing the unhelpful beliefs that lead to negative emotions

Abraham Lincoln[5] said, 'Most people are about as happy as they make their minds up to be.'

We would say remember the importance of being needed, of feeling that you are making a difference. Make sure that at least some of your goals are worthwhile and that they tie in with your beliefs and your meaning.

Show that you're happy! There are few things in life more contagious. Let it affect as many people as you can – it's not a cake with just enough to go around.

Emotional Intelligence

We have referred to Emotional Intelligence a few times already in this chapter. Not too long ago, IQ, the intelligence quotient, was just about the only measure that people paid any attention to. IQ refers to a person's knowledge, memory and reasoning ability when scored against a standard comparative measure through the completion of a set test. But IQ forms just part of the intelligence picture. There are a myriad of subtleties around a person's overall ability and aptitude that a pure IQ test cannot identify or rate. More recent academic studies have identified human attributes and personality components that, combined with IQ, better determine true potential.[6] The emergence of Emotional Intelligence, referred to as EI or EQ, incorporates the softer, interpersonal skills and emotionally based talents that add temperament and character to personal aptitude.

Of course, we all have the ability to increase our EQ and, with it, our effectiveness due to Neuroplasticity, which we covered in Chapter 3. These are exactly the skills that are built through Mind Fitness. You're learning to enhance your EQ by reading this book.

Although there are several academic definitions of EQ, there are key areas of crossover. These are the common components:

▶ **Self and social awareness** – you are aware of and realistic about your own emotions. Do you rise to anger easily? Would you say that you're a jealous type? Distrustful? Do you become easily anxious in adversity? Do you react well to constructive feedback and not default to personalisation leading to feelings of hurt? Do you know your strengths? Your weaknesses? Do you understand how your qualities affect others? What are your goals? What are your values? Are your goals in line with your values?

▶ **Social skills** – your ability to interact and engage cooperatively with others. Can you effectively influence people to work collectively and to move in your direction? Do you understand what motivates others? Do you use your social skills to develop productive relationships?

▶ **Self-regulation** – do you use your heightened self-awareness to reframe your unhelpful emotions? Does that help you to think and take control before you speak, to resist acting immediately on knee-jerk emotional impulses? Adaptability is a highly valuable personal asset.

The comedian Craig Ferguson set out a checklist of three simple questions. Think:

▶ Does this need to be said?
▶ Does this need to be said by me?
▶ Does this need to be said by me now?

This very insightful approach can save so much upset and regret.

▶ **Motivation** – the will to act and the drive to succeed. Not at any price or in any way, though. That's where empathy is so important.

▶ **Empathy** – understanding the views and feelings of others. How would I feel in their shoes? What would motivate me if I were them in this situation? What is it I need to say now to make a difference? How would I like to be treated in these circumstances?

All these are skills you will have been developing through the book. As you enhance your EQ, you open a new door to a more effective, less stressful life. You'll find that you're better able to accept criticism and use it to your advantage to affect positive change. You'll become more authentic, adhering to your principals because you develop a greater understanding of your values and personal goals. You become the best version of you. You learn how to successfully *Unlock You*!

Awareness of Self

Awareness of self is key to any significant changes. The problem often is not our unhelpful beliefs – we know how to change them using the ABC Model – but our lack of awareness of them.

Take a moment to be aware of all the patterns that have occurred in your life. We are likely to have made the same mistakes over and over again, partly because of our cognitive bias and expectations that caused us to choose badly in the first place, and partly because it has become our habitual behaviour, our route of least resistance.

Exercise 11.7: The You That Others See

Choose three people that you trust and explain to them that it's extremely important that they are honest.

Ask them how they see you. If they were going to describe you to a good friend of theirs, what would they say?

Write the description down so that you can think about it afterwards.

This is sometimes an uncomfortable exercise because the way that others see us can be a fair distance from the way we see ourselves, but it's well worth doing. It may be that there are positive qualities that you had not expected or realised that you possess and, if there are negative aspects, it gives you the opportunity to change the way you speak and behave. You can work to change the way you respond to other people, to bring their image into line with the positive Self-Image you are working towards and the person you want to be.

Awareness of Others

Awareness of others can help our journey to a happier state in a number of ways.

As we've said, we often expect people to react and respond to circumstances in the same way as us. Life becomes a whole lot easier if we realise that, in most cases, when there is conflict, the other person is not trying to make us suffer, they simply understand and interpret the situation differently from us. It is their truth. If we can credit them for being sincere, it gives us a fighting chance of coming to a shared understanding. It's good to ask ourselves, 'How does this appear to her?', 'How does she feel about this?'

Being aware of others guides us to an understanding that is essential in building and sustaining relationships. Most breakdowns of relationships, personal and professional, come at least in part from miscommunication and misunderstanding.

Try to keep the big picture in your mind; care about the result rather than who's right.

Exercise 11.8: Deep Listening

In Mind Fitness, we call listening with effort and energy 'attending'.

Part A – choose a conversation that you are going to have with someone during the day. It's best if it is someone you know fairly well but who isn't a very close friend.

Really listen to what they say, ask questions to find out more.

Afterwards, write down what you know about them/learned about them.

Part B – choose a conversation that you are going to have during the day with a close friend or relative.

Really listen to what they say.

It's likely that you won't have updated your opinion of them and the way you see them and respond to them for a very long time.

Afterwards, write down what surprised you/what you learned about them that was new.

Exercise 11.9: Walking in Their Shoes

Close your eyes and spend one minute considering a recent event or situation that has happened to someone that you know well. Now play through the event in your mind, as if it is happening to you.

If you have time, speak this 'story' out loud or write it down, still using the first person 'I ... '.

It's a great exercise for the development of empathy as well as awareness.

Questions and Answers

▶ **How do I know if what I mean by happy is the same as anyone else?**

What you mean by happy one day in one situation will not be the same as what you mean by happy in another situation, so, yes, it is likely that another person's version of the emotion will be different again. But perhaps that doesn't really matter. We can tell if another person is feeling sadness or joy and we can still play our part in helping them to have a positive experience.

▶ **If I have experienced extreme negative emotions, will I always be prone to experiencing them again?**

As with any experience, once we have had it, the engram is established in our brain and there is a neural pathway. It is a route we have travelled. If we have experienced that negative emotion many times, it may have become a habitual path.

We can make the change as with any other by developing new habits and building new pathways. It's not easy if it's a route that had been emotionally charged but it's absolutely possible. Try to make as many changes as you can to your lifestyle, altering habits and behaviours that, in your mind, are linked to the emotion.

If you know that the first time you felt depressed you were living in a rural village, perhaps make it easier for yourself by staying in the city for the period that you make the change, and use Adaptive Behaviour as much as you can. Begin new activities in new places, if this is possible. Surround yourself with new people and new ideas. Think about the things that give you a feeling of support and make sure these are built into your life.

Most important, be aware but not fearful. Know that you are strong. Expect the best but know that, if the worst came, you would experience it in the moment and come through it. You have done so before.

Conclusion

Some Mind Fitness workshop attendees express concern that, if they move from UNEs to HNEs, if they, say, lose their anger and aggression, they'll end up being doormats to strong-minded or difficult people. The absolute opposite is true. By utilising HNEs, we can stay in control and form considered, rational, assertive responses to life's challenges. Having the ability to apply HNEs instead of defaulting to UNEs is, quite simply, a life changer. It takes a little time and practice to go from intellectual understanding to emotionally embedding your new responses, but the day you realise that you've automatically responded in a considered, rational, measured way to something that previously would have caused you upset is a day of personal liberation.

This is the chapter in which we have looked at happiness. Key to remember is that acting positively will make you feel positive. Have a day when you determine to be cheerful and kind to everyone you meet; act only with compassion; think only with compassion.

Through the Mind Fitness process, one thing that is certain to become stronger is your capacity to enjoy life. Remember that you don't enjoy anything unless you are paying attention to it. Don't let the good stuff pass you by; think about how differently the chocolate tasted when you were eating it mindfully. Look around your house. There is probably a host of objects that are connected to memories. Take a minute to recall each one and why you wanted to buy it or how it was given to you. There is no point in having these things if you do not enjoy them.

And remember not to judge yourself or others. A mistake does not require an emotional response – only a course-correct.

12

Enjoy your life

How to make this a simple enjoyable part of your life

You were drawn to this book because you want to change. This is an incredible opportunity. Don't plan to change tomorrow, do it now. Remember this is all about achieving your potential and enjoying your life. If you love to dance – dance! It may not be an opportunity available to you next year or the year after that. We have to value, to give meaning, to the time that we have. Don't spend the night watching TV and wishing you were doing something else. Choose everything more carefully, more mindfully – good books, good TV, good chocolate.

The commitment to change is the crux in any story of lives turned round on whatever level, from total transformation to minor positive boost. It's as important as the process itself. We all know the old adage that insanity is the insistence on doing the same thing over and over while hoping for a different result. And, yet, we do it all the time. Everything in this book has guided you towards breaking this pattern, making the commitment to change happen. And it is natural, everything changes, all the time. Resistance is futile! Embracing the concept of change, of continual change, gives you almost unlimited opportunity and places you in sync with the natural world. You can be in the moment, you can respond in a simple non-melodramatic way. Life becomes an adventure because every conversation is an opportunity.

When we first begin the process of change, we feel as though we are relaxing our grip on life. A little way in, we realise we are actually taking up the reins. The sensation of being in control of our lives, perhaps for the first time, is extraordinary. Of course, there will be days when this journey doesn't go so well, but hey, today is just today; course-correct.

To keep changing is to keep learning. Accept that the paradigm of how you think the world works is going to be broken as you learn new things. Make it a habit to learn and to be inspired by successful and inspiring people. Be open to all that others can give you. To do this means accepting other people's 'otherness', itself an invigorating and broadening process. And, wherever you can, try to be the one that is helping, nurturing, teaching. Focussing on a purpose beyond yourself will help you to keep the drive and motivation. Try to reflect or model the change that you would like to see in the world.

Reminders and tips

Be friends with your brain – be as aware of that monumental piece of equipment as you can be. Use the mindfulness exercises to gain focus and concentration. Notice thoughts that concern you or turn up uninvited, but do not let the ANTs invade. The mind acts like an enemy for those who don't control it.

Self-Image – don't let self-doubt creep in; it's a weapon that you are turning on yourself. Be particularly vigilant when you have had a difficult day or you are tired.

Thinking Errors – keep working to reframe your Thinking Errors. Don't awfulise, be vigilant in asking yourself 'how awful is it really?' And don't procrastinate, step outside your comfort zone to do what needs to be done. Stop things hanging over you by using the 4Ds for each task – Done/Deleted/Deferred/Delegated. Let the doing become the habit, your most travelled path.

Gratitude – when people are grateful, they are noticeably more productive. Train yourself to stop noticing what you don't have and start noticing what you do have.

Positivity – train your brain to see obstacles as challenges; dealing positively with these often give the most reward as they deepen your experience of the process and provide a powerful sense of achievement. Let go of that part of you that is cushioning yourself for disappointment. It is holding you back. Instead, catch your dreams. Congratulate yourself on them. Be proud of them. Remember to keep recognising your successes and celebrating them, and remember to look outwards. Look for potential in others and it will help you to recognise it in yourself.

Beliefs and Meaning – check in with your meaning as often as you can and remember to tie your goals, beliefs and meaning together as closely as possible. Gain awareness of as many of your beliefs as possible and be as honest as you can when deciding whether or not they are helpful. And remember, if any of your beliefs are causing you to beat yourself with a stick of your own making, you're probably beating other people with it too.

Goals – in the chapter on goals, we stressed the need to set attainable goals. This does involve some managing of expectations. But remember that managing is not about lowering them; it just involves thinking about them clearly. Don't strive for goals that would never make you happy.

Focus – don't let the ANTs steal your brain. If you feel the downward spiral of negative thoughts begin, do a mindfulness exercise. And remember that you won't enjoy anything unless you are paying attention to it.

Empathise – put yourself in the shoes of other people as often as possible.

Remember to use the ABC

Here is a quick example to remind you of the process – an ABC of email conflict. It's something that comes up a lot on the courses we run.

With Rigid Demands

A Activating Event

Dawn had simply had enough. Work colleague Jon had sent another email bomb, copying in the world again, presenting Dawn and her team in a very bad light, diverting, she felt, his own failings.

B Belief

How dare you send this email, you idiot. You must not criticise me or my team in this public forum. Or, indeed, at all! No one tries to make me look a fool and gets away with it. I must not be made to feel a fool.

C Consequence

She flips and immediately sends a response to Jon in a very forthright manner. Every point made is responded to in the strongest and most emotive of terms. Once she's satisfied that she has all the areas covered, she presses 'copy all'. 'Let the email war commence' she thinks.

Emotional – Anger, anxiety, hurt

Behavioural – Knee-jerk reaction in sending a hastily written, highly reactive, emotionally-laden response that will, inevitably, continue the dispute.

Physiological – Pounding heart, head hurting, tearful.

With Preferences

A Activating Event

Dawn had simply had enough. Work colleague Jon had sent another email bomb, copying the world again, presenting Dawn and her team in a very bad light, diverting, she felt, his own failings.

B Belief

How tedious. I would prefer that Jon didn't do this, but I know that he has a reputation of using email in this way.

C Consequence

Emotional – Healthy anger, concern, sorrow.

Behavioural – Dawn takes some time to re-read the email. She notes down the points made and determines a response to each, based on facts, not anger. Once she has all the facts and evidence to hand, she goes to see Jon. That rather catches him off guard and Dawn then calmly, but assertively, takes Jon through each point, giving her own perspective. Together, Dawn and Jon agree a way forward and a suitable solution to each point. Dawn then sends an email to all those copied in the original, itemising each point and the solutions agreed.

Physiological – Dawn is fine. Feeling a little sad maybe. Confrontation is never her favourite thing. But as it's measured and on her terms; her head feels OK and her heartrate is normal.

Conclusion

It's vitally important that this process of change never feels like a chore. Love the journey that you are on. If it ever feels like a slog, then stop and hold yourself to account, because it's how you *feel* that counts.

If you are writing down that you are grateful for something but not feeling it, break off, be aware; go and make a cup of tea. There will be things in your life that are challenging, difficult, but you are greater than your circumstances. Stay positive about the journey and your ability to make it happen, and that will power you to make the best decisions you can when the obstacles come along.

Let the change deepen inside you. Gradually, you will move from practising it to living it. You will learn to speak the language of your practice and you will be speaking from the heart.

Remember that this is a change that will strengthen your abilities to look outwards, to build relationships, to connect. It is not about spending time on the self – you are developing your abilities to be a strong, dynamic part of your family, your community and the wider world, and you cannot spend time more wisely than that. The new you will be able to invest meaning, make changes and make people happy.

Focus in on what you love and love doing. Whatever you choose to focus on expands in your life (which is a good reason not to focus on the things that you hate).

Happiness is not a myth or something we should relegate to stories for children. As we have said before, we think better, perform better and are healthier when we are happy. Research shows that happy people are good at relationships, at gratitude, philanthropy, optimism, living in the present, staying physically active and maintaining a commitment to goals. *You can acquire the habit of happiness.*

We are conditioned, in the West, to think that life should somehow be a struggle, that, if it does not feel almost impossible, then we are not trying hard enough. I (BW) don't know why – I can think of no way to more surely waste a life. Through the Mind Fitness process, this mindset will melt away. I don't know when it happened for me, but I can honestly say that I have never been happier. It's not a constant euphoria, of course, it's a deep-seated contentment. I feel awake and connected. There have been times in my life when I have had more (a husband and parents), but it doesn't feel that way. I feel as if I have so much, an incredible daughter, a fantastic inclusive theatre company, the Mind Fitness courses and this book.

Andy feels the same way. Believe me, he is not a sentimentalist. His god is science; he gets angry about politics almost every day and he's certainly an optimist by process of change rather than predisposition. But he's happy. Once you have guided your thoughts over a period of time, you simply start living the life.

Live until you die, embrace change, make life! Whatever your beliefs about whether this is our only shot, it is certainly too good an opportunity to miss. Let's set out to be calm, confident, kind and authentic, to enjoy this amazing life. Let's make it count.

Six-week follow-up programme

Now you're ready for the six-week follow-up programme. By the end of the six weeks, and with the work you have already done, you will have embedded the new practice into your way of thinking and daily routine. As with any fitness commitment, the practice has to be maintained, but it will have become part of your habitual behaviour – built into the way you think – it will be your route of least resistance.

Each day focusses on a different aspect of the course and we've ordered them so that they are easy to remember. This focus is set out to be done in the evening, but, if it works better for you to swap it round and do this at the beginning of the day, that's fine.

Monday – Mindfulness

Tuesday – Change

Wednesday – Worry Less

Thursday – Think better

Friday – Feel positive

The rest of the day is simple practice of the key elements and these stay the same so that you have an easy-to-remember routine. You don't need to be glued to the book and, most importantly, the fundamentals quickly become your most travelled pathway. These include a few check-ins that you do every day.

The weekends are about being creative and having fun. The amount of times we hear people say, 'I can keep myself on track during the week, but at the weekend it all goes to pot!' You should never feel like that about anything! If that's the way you feel, then you are on the wrong diet or exercise routine, or the wrong course. There's nothing in the world that you will stick to if it doesn't make you feel better. That's not to say that sometimes things (including the process of change) will feel like a challenge, but it should always, as you work through, make you feel better – not self-righteous, better!

You'll see that there are two weekend days set out; it doesn't matter which way round you do them.

Tuesday Change centres on tackling the ABCs and you'll notice that these are reinforced through the Wednesday and Thursday exercises. Once you have engaged with whatever unhelpful belief you are currently challenging for the three days, it will be an embedded part of your thinking through the rest of the week.

Each day is set out for week 1. From week 2, we show only the changes.

Each week, from 1–6, your practice deepens. The separate parts of the process become more closely woven together.

We suggest you keep your notebook to hand to write down any issues that emerge, as well as any thoughts or ideas.

Good luck!

Week 1

Monday
Daily Practice with a Focus on Mindfulness

Morning

1 Begin the day with Image Breathing – two minutes

2 Positive Affirmation – your mantra of Self-Image – two minutes

During the day

In times of stress or anxiety, use one of the following:

▶ NOW (page 19)

▶ Reframing a Demand to a Preference – 'I would prefer that …

▶ Using the Awfulising technique – asking yourself on a scale of 1–10 how awful is this really?

▶ Power Poses (page 118)

Also take notice of:

▶ Relationships – make sure you are watching, listening, empathising, not taking situations personally

▶ Any unhelpful beliefs

Evening

1 Monday Mindfulness:

    ▶ This week do the Circles of Attention exercise (page xvii)

    ▶ Notice any thoughts and then let them go

2 Make a note of:

    ▶ Anything that disturbed you through the day

    ▶ Any times you had to say 'I would prefer that …'

    ▶ Any situations you had to scale down using the Awfulising technique

3 Congratulate yourself for all of these

4 Gratitude – make a note of three things you are grateful for

Tuesday
Daily Practice with a Focus on Change

Morning

1   Begin the day with Image Breathing – two minutes

2   Positive Affirmation – your mantra of Self-Image – two minutes

During the day

In times of stress or anxiety, use one of the following:

▶   NOW (page 19)

▶   Reframing a Demand to a Preference – 'I would prefer that ...

▶   Using the Awfulising technique – asking yourself on a scale of 1–10 how awful is this really?

▶   Power Poses (page 118)

Also take notice of:

▶   Relationships – make sure you are watching, listening, empathising, not taking situations personally

▶   Any unhelpful beliefs

Evening

1   Tuesday Change – working on ABC thinking

Perhaps you are already aware of an unhelpful belief that you want to change. If not, spend a minute or two identifying one

Work through this belief using the Disputing Form from Chapter 4 (page 54)

2   Make a note of:

▶   anything that disturbed you through the day

▶   any times you had to say 'I would prefer that ...'

▶   any situations you had to scale down using the Awfulising technique.

Congratulate yourself for all of these

3   Gratitude – make a note of three things you are grateful for

Wednesday
Daily Practice with a Focus on Worrying Less

Morning

1 Begin the day with Image Breathing – two minutes

2 Positive Affirmation – your mantra of Self-Image – two minutes

During the day

In times of stress or anxiety, use one of the following:

▶ NOW (page 19)

▶ Reframing a Demand to a Preference – 'I would prefer that ...'

▶ Using the Awfulising technique – asking yourself on a scale of 1–10 how awful is this really?

▶ Power Poses (page 118)

Also take notice of:

▶ Relationships – make sure you are watching, listening, empathising, not taking situations personally

▶ Any unhelpful beliefs

Evening

1 Worry less:

   ▶ First check in with your ABC goal that you set out on Tuesday

   ▶ Write down two things that you are worrying about connected to this unhelpful belief

▶ Go through the reframing exercise 'Awfulising' using the scale of 1–10 (page 80)

   ▶ Now ask yourself – How persuasive is it? – How permanent is it? – How personal is it?

   ▶ Do a one-minute exercise visualising how you may reflect back on the problem in one year's time

➔

2 Make a note of:

- ▶ Anything that disturbed you through the day
- ▶ Any times you had to say 'I would prefer that ...'
- ▶ Any situations you had to scale down using the awfulising technique

3 Congratulate yourself for all of these

4 Gratitude – make a note of three things you are grateful for

Thursday
Daily Practice with a Focus on Thinking Better

Morning

1 Begin the day with Image Breathing – two minutes

2 Positive Affirmation – your mantra of Self-Image – two minutes

During the day

In times of stress or anxiety, use one of the following:

- ▶ NOW (page 19)
- ▶ Reframing a Demand to a Preference – 'I would prefer that ...
- ▶ Using the Awfulising technique – asking yourself on a scale of 1–10 how awful is this really?
- ▶ Power Poses (page 118)

Also take notice of:

- ▶ Relationships – make sure you are watching, listening, empathising, not taking situations personally
- ▶ Any unhelpful beliefs

Evening

1 Think Better:

- ▶ First check in with the ABC goal you set out on Tuesday

▶ Next, we are going to work on a Thinking Error. If you think there is one that ties in with the unhelpful belief you are challenging, pick that one. If not, pick one that you know you use. See if you can remember any moments this week where that Thinking Error has got in your way or caused you a level of distress.

▶ Now do the Thinking Error exercise on page 81

2 Make a note of:

▶ Anything that disturbed you through the day

▶ Any times you had to say 'I would prefer that…'

▶ Any situations you had to scale down using the awfulising technique

3 Congratulate yourself for all of these

4 Gratitude – make a note of three things you are grateful for

---

Friday
Daily Practice with a Focus on Feeling Positive

Morning

1 Begin the day with Image Breathing – two minutes

2 Positive Affirmation – your mantra of Self-Image – two minutes

During the day

In times of stress or anxiety, use one of the following:

▶ NOW (page 19)

▶ Reframing a Demand to a Preference – 'I would prefer that…'

▶ Using the Awfulising technique – asking yourself on a scale of 1–10 'how awful is this really?'

▶ Power Poses (page 118)

Also take notice of:

▶ Relationships – make sure you are watching, listening, empathising, not taking situations personally

▶ Any unhelpful beliefs

➔

Evening – *You will notice that the order is different on a Friday.*

1   Make a note of:

> ▶ Anything that disturbed you through the day

> ▶ Any times you had to say 'I would prefer that...'

> ▶ Any situations you had to scale down using the awfulising technique

Congratulate yourself for all of these

2   Feel Positive: remember that feeling positive is about how you see yourself and how you see the world

> ▶ Self-Image – find three things to congratulate yourself for. Spend a minute or so thinking about each one

> ▶ Compassion – spend a minute or two thinking about someone you care about deeply. Don't spend it worrying about them (even if they're your children), Just let yourself take notice of how wonderful they are

> ▶ Gratitude – make a note of three things you are grateful for – today spend a minute or so really thinking about how great they make you feel

---

Weekend – Day 1
Being Creative and Checking in with your Goals

Morning

1   Begin the day with Image Breathing followed by a Body Scan (page 108)

2   Positive Affirmation – your mantra of Self-Image

During the day

Choose any one of the Creative Exercises from Chapter 9

Evening

Check in with your Goals. Update the list you made in Chapter 5. Congratulate yourself for any that have been achieved or for significant progress towards them. Make sure that you add the Goal of Changing your Belief in accordance with the ABC challenge you set on Tuesday.

Weekend – Day 2
Being Creative and Adaptive

Morning

1   Begin the day by listening to a piece of music – really listening. Pick out each instrument, the pauses. If it has vocals, be aware of the shape and weight of the words

2   Follow this with a piece of new learning – it can be anything at all – google something you are interested in. Look up a place on a map

During the day

Go for a walk – do the Walking Exercise from page 147

Evening – Exercising the Imagination

1   Exercise – Foxhole in my Mind – (page 24) build in as much detail as you can. Really feel the thrill of being in the special place

2   Exercise – do a Goal-Based Visualisation (page 66). Either use the Goal that you are working on in your current ABC challenge or one of the Goals you thought about yesterday. Really exercise your imagination – concentrate on the detail and the emotions you feel as you imagine

---

Weeks 2–6

For weeks 2–6, the 'Morning' and 'During the day' activities remain the same. The evening's designated exercise changes to broaden and deepen your experience of the process through this period. It is also structured so that the different areas of the programme increasingly overlap and feed into each other, so that it is cemented as a unified and cohesive way of thinking, feeling and responding.

By the time you are half-way through the process, it is much less about how you are doing the exercises and much more about how you are living your life. It's not just a way of thinking, it's a way of living. Your intuition and instinctive response will be working for you, and your default position will be helpful. You and your brain will be great friends and, like any good friend, it will be there to support you and to help you enjoy your life.

Week 2 (Awareness)

Monday Mindfulness

Do the Body Scan from page 108

Notice any parts of the body in which there is tension or a heightened sensory awareness.

Tuesday Change

Exactly as you did on Tuesday of week 1, choose a belief that you want to challenge, complete the Form and begin the process.

Wednesday Worry Less

First check in with the ABC thinking that you filled in yesterday. Was it something that you thought about during the day?

Make a note of anything you have worried about today. Consider the cause of the worry in terms of your response to the situation or adversity. Go through each of the situations saying, 'I would prefer that ... but ...'.

Thursday Think Better

Today we are looking at Low Frustration Tolerance, a massively common Thinking Error. Identify the most recent situation in which you have exhibited this. Use the three questions in Chapter 6 to reframe this intolerance.

Friday Feel Positive

Self-Image – do the Big I Little I exercise on page 95. Make sure you write at least 10 little I's. Read each Little I out loud, taking a moment to smile and feel proud.

Weekend – Day 1

Consider the Goals you revisited on the weekend of week 1. Do a Goal-Based Visualisation for the one that is most important to you. This exercise is on page 66.

Pick any creative exercise from Chapter 9.

Weekend – Day 2

Revisit the meaning that you considered in the early chapters of this book. Does it still hold good? Does it inspire you? If not, make any necessary changes.

Think about three things that you have done or are doing to ensure that this meaning has a dominant place in your life.

Week 3 (Emotions)

Monday Mindfulness

Do the Mindful Eating Exercise from page 148

Afterwards, commit to eating this way as often as you can during the coming week. Note the way that it makes your body feel. Note any emotions that it brings forward.

Tuesday Change

First revisit the beliefs that you set out to change on the Tuesdays of weeks 1 and 2. How far through the process of change would you say that you are on each of these? As long as you think that these two beliefs are starting to move, for example that you are starting to shift from intellectual understanding to emotional understanding, then begin working on a third belief. If not, then continue working with the two you have already selected. Create a Positive Affirmation linked to each of the new beliefs. Try to capture the emotion you will feel when this new belief has been successfully embedded in your life.

Wednesday Worry Less

Worrying less is about developing the positive as well as challenging the negative aspects of your life. Make a list of five helpful beliefs that you have and spend a minute thinking about each. Consider the positive impact each has on your life.

Thursday Think Better

Today we are going to challenge Selective Thinking, something we all fall prey to. One of the most common things that we do is to discount the positive. Consider one issue or problem that you are having to deal with at the moment. It can be personal or work-related. Make a scattergram, just jotting down all the various aspects of the situation, big or small. Then consider each in turn, focussing on any positives; for example, perhaps you have done something similar in the past that went well, have at least one or two good people to help you, and have meaning invested in the achievement or resolution.

Friday Feel Positive

Gratitude – make a list of five things that you are grateful for.

Now, by each, write why you are grateful – use detail if you have time.

Finally, go through writing the way that each of the five make you feel. Try to capture the emotion, really feel it as you write it down.

Weekend – Day 1
Revisit the Goals, Meaning and Belief you thought about in weeks 1 and 2. Choose the Goal that makes you most excited (not necessarily the one that you would say was most important.)

Do a Goal-Based Visualisation for this Goal (see page 66), really concentrating on the emotion.

Weekend – Day 2
Choose one of the Creative Exercises from Chapter 9 or simply do something creative – paint a picture, write a poem or choreograph a dance in your kitchen.

Afterwards, make a note of how creating makes you feel. Try to capture the emotion and hold it as you write it down.

Week 4 (Connecting)

Monday Mindfulness
Go for a Mindful Walk, preferably in a setting that you really enjoy, as on page 147.

Note any people that you see or meet along the way and smile. If you can, spend a moment imagining them in a positive situation.

Tuesday Change
By now, you will have at least two beliefs that you are currently working to change. Last week, we spent a lot of time concentrating on emotions so, today, we're going to apply this to the beliefs you are working through. Think about the Unhealty Negative Emotions that used to be associated with each of your old unhelpful beliefs. Now think about the new healthier emotions that are evoked by, or are forming as a result of, your new more helpful beliefs. Write these down. Try to capture the emotion as you do so.

Wednesday Worry Less
The activity for today and Friday are linked. One of the proven ways to worry less about your personal situation is to be strongly connected with others and the wider world, the bigger picture.

Spend a few minutes drawing a little galaxy chart, with you in the centre and circles all around you, each representing a person or area of your life with which you have a connection.

Now draw a (preferably coloured) line, joining you with any that involve you feeling compassion or having a similar positive emotional investment.

Over the next two days, be as aware of these connections as you can, even when they only briefly cross your mind.

Thursday Think Better
As with many of this week's exercises, we are going to concentrate on the way we connect or, in this case, the way that we perceive that we connect. We're going to work on that Thinking Error that causes much unnecessary angst and wasted time – Personalisation. We all take things personally that were never intended that way, and it's especially easy to do when we are struggling with other parts of our lives. It's easier to tackle, however, when we are thinking and feeling positively about how we relate to the external world, which is the focus of this week's activities.

Make a note of three occasions in the last month when you have felt that you were personally under attack. Spend a minute on each, looking at the situation through the eyes of the other person involved. Walk in their shoes, as we did in Chapter11.

Friday Feel Positive
Compassion – Make a list of all the times this week that you have felt compassion. Hopefully, a lot of these will be linked to the connections that you identified on Wednesday, but it can also include compassion you felt for someone whose story you heard about on the news or the plight of a friend who you know only indirectly.

By each line of the list, write a number denoting the level of compassion you feel or felt on a scale of one to ten. Now choose three and think about each for a minute, considering how you could push the number up a notch or two.

Weekend – Day 1
Goals, Beliefs, Meaning.

Consider the roles that other people play in your most important goals, in your most positive beliefs and, most importantly, in the parts of your life in which you invest meaning.

Focus for a minute or two on the way that these people make you feel.

Weekend – Day 2
Collective Creative.

If you possibly can, try to do something in which you and another will be creating together. Enter into a role play with your child or children, or persuade a friend to do the adaptive drawing exercise outlined on page 124. If that's not possible, do something creative in which you are using a stimulus provided by another person. Rewrite a poem, using the first line of one that's already written, envisage a video game that is a spin-off of an existing one, sing along to a well known record, but make up your own words!

Week 5 (Courage)

Monday Mindfulness
This exercise is called Back to Centre. Stand straight, feet shoulder width apart and arms by your side, but without tension. Close your eyes and take in the feeling of being perfectly balanced, of being 'on centre'.

Move each of your arms, then your shoulders, then flex your knees so that the hips move, then move your head and neck. Each time, bring the body part back to neutral, experiencing the feeling of being back on centre. Keep your focus on the part of the body that is moving. Bring your attention back when it wanders. Move through each body part two to three times. Get a strong sense of your strength and courage every time you come back to centre.

Tuesday Change
Take a new and more challenging Belief to work on – something you never thought you'd be able to change! Fill out a new Form with as much excitement as you can.

Wednesday Worry Less
Make a list of the Beliefs and Thinking Errors that you have reframed or are in the process of reframing. Read through the list with a full sense of the courage you have shown and the strength you have used to effect this change.

Then make a list of 10 scary things that you can't wait to do!

Thursday Think Better

Make a list of all the times that you can recall since you began this book where you have changed a rigid demand for a preference – every situation in which you have checked your response and said, 'I would prefer that ... but ...'.

Now put a tick by any of these that are situations in which it has taken strength or courage to deal with the situation showing positivity and grace.

Friday feel positive

Spend a while searching for inspiring quotes about courage and bravery. Read through them, preferably out loud, really feeling their intent, making them your own.

Weekend – Day 1

Take six photos that you have (either hard copy or on your phone) and creatively link them together to make a story about courage. Either write the story down or tell it to a family member or friend.

Weekend – Day 2

Draw three circles. Write down in one a major Goal that you have, in the second an important Belief that you hold and in the third your Meaning. Use these as a stimulus for a poem, story or drawing. It can be as simple or as complex as you like.

Week 6 (Pulling it all together and checking in)

Monday Mindfulness Check-in

Choose three mindfulness or mindfulness-based exercises from anywhere in the book and do them one after the other.

Make a note of which one you think works best for you and why, and also a note of which you enjoy the most.

Write a note on how you feel after the one you enjoy most and after the one you think is having the most effect.

Tuesday Change Check-in

Make a list of the six changes relating to any aspects of the programme that are having the most positive effect on your life.

Write a list of all the Beliefs you have changed or are in the process of changing. Rate each one according to how far through the process of change you feel yourself to be −10 is a completed change and 1 a small step along the way.

Wednesday Worry Less Check-in
Make a list of the different techniques you now use to worry less, to keep your stress level down. Note which ones work best for you.

Worrying less amounts to:

- ▶ Worrying less often
- ▶ Worry less intensely
- ▶ Feeling able to cope with whatever it is that is worrying you

Think for a few minutes about how you are doing on each count; if one area is lagging behind, decide on a couple of steps that you can take to catch up.

Thursday Think Better Check-in
Choose three Thinking Errors (detailed in Chapter 6) that you feel you now resort to less often. List three positive consequences, three ways in which the change has impacted positively on your life.

Friday Feel Positive Check-in
Make a list of the recent occasions in which you have stepped outside your comfort zone. Congratulate yourself for each. This is a key part of the process. Between your comfort zone and your panic zone is the Zone of Proximal Development and this is the place where we really learn. It's often called the Stretch Zone because we want to expand it wherever we can. You can bet, with all the work that you have done through the book, that your Stretch Zone will have been well and truly stretched! And so the whole process of learning and continuing this change becomes easier.

Finish off with a Goal-Based Visualisation (page 66) imagining this procedure of stretch in either a real or abstract way, to cement the process.

Weekend – Day 1
First choose one exercise from the book – perhaps your favourite one that you particularly enjoy.

Then go through the book, writing out any quotes you like, notes, ideas or reminders onto separate pieces of paper. Post these around the house or your room (or office) as feels right. For example, the motivational ones might be placed where they will be most needed.

Weekend – Day 2
The last day of the six weeks and you are going to create a Vision Board with a difference. Rather than focussing on what you want to have (or achieve in the conventional sense), it will have at its centre what you want to be.

Take a piece of board (corkboard to pin things on or cardboard to stick things on – yep, this is old school!). At the centre, place a representation of the *Unlocked You*; for example, this could be an outline with all the big changes written inside it. Round the *Unlocked You* place pictures that represent your most important Goals, Beliefs and Meaning.

Now make different areas on the board for everything else that has been important to the process and is important to the direction in which you are headed – perhaps your family and friends, other goals and ambitions, places you would like to travel to, things you would like to learn about. Only put on the things you feel strongly and positively about, and add in a few inspirational quotes.

Place it somewhere important and easily visible; get into the habit of noticing what is on it and smiling. You have done brilliantly so far and this is a good reminder that it is *all* to play for.

Notes

Introduction

[1] Dietrich, A. (2004) The cognitive neuroscience of creativity. Available at: https://www.ncbi.nlm.nih.gov/pubmed/15875970.

[2] Costandi, M. (2016) *Neuroplasticity*.

[3] LONI (Laboratory of Neuro Imaging) then attached to UCLA, now to University of Southern California, has estimated 60,000–70,000; School of Medicine (2011) estimated 60,000–80,000; National Science Foundation (2005) estimated 12,000–60,000.

[4] Egan, M. F. (2007) *Chemical Reactions*. National Institute of Health. Available at: https://www.ncbi.nlm.nih.gov/books/NBK20369/.

[5] Harvard Medical School (Sara Lazar, 2005 and 2010); Leiden University, Netherlands (Lorenza Colzato, 2012); University of Texas, Austin (Kristin Neff and Christopher Germer, 2012); University of Massachusetts (Dr Britta Holzel and James Carmody, 2011).

Chapter 1

[1] Frankl, V. (1946) *Man's Search for Meaning*.

Chapter 2

[1] 100 billion neurons in Herculano-Houzel, S. (2009) 'The human brain in numbers': A linearly scaled-up primate brain. Available at: https://www.ncbi.nlm.nih.gov/pmc/articles/PMC2776484/

[2] Albert Ellis, Founder of REBT.

[3] Anokhin, P. K *Biology and Neurophysiology of the Conditioned Reflex and Its Role in Adaptive Behavior*. Pavlov, I. (1890) *Classical Conditioning*.

[4] Durham Veterans Affairs Medical Centre (Rajendra A Morey, 2012).

[5] R A Bressan (2005), University of Sao Paulo.

[6] Kurzwell, R (2012) *How to Create a Mind*.

Chapter 3

[1] Garland, E. (2009) *Neuroplasticity, Psychosocial Genomics, and the Biopsychosocial Paradigm in the 21st Century*. Florida: Florida State University.

[2] Eriksson, P. S. (1998) *Neurogenesis in the adult human hippocampus*.

[3] Albert Ellis, Founder of REBT.

[4] UTSW Medical Centre, Dr Thomas Sudhof (Nobel Prize Winner).

[5] Kar, N. 'CBT for the treatment of PTSD: A review'. Available at: https://www.ncbi.nlm.nih.gov/pmc/articles/PMC3083990/.

[6] Carla Shatz, Stanford University (2013).

Chapter 4

[1] Albert Ellis, founder of REBT.

Chapter 5

[1] Hill, N. (1937) *Think and Grow Rich*.

[2] *New Scientist*, Volume 172.

Chapter 6

1.   Aaron T. Beck, founder of CBT, University of Pennsylvania
2.   Aaron T. Beck, founder of CBT, University of Pennsylvania

Chapter 7

1.   Drs Richard Davidson and Jon Kabat-Zinn (study in 2003).
2.   Lazarus A A (1977) *Towards an Egoless State of Being.*

Chapter 8

1.   René Descartes, seventeenth-century French philosopher.
2.   Jarrett, C. 'Great myths of the brain' Available at: http://www.bbc.com/future/story/20141118-how-many-senses-do-you-have.
3.   Dr Gershon, M. (1998) *The Second Brain.*
4.   Prof. Ted Kaptchuk, Harvard-affiliated Beth Israel Deaconess Medical Centre (2014).
5.   G. D. Jacobs (2004).
6.   Amaro, A. *Holistic Living - Dharma Talks.*
7.   Cuddy, A J.C. and Carney, D. R (2012) *The Benefit of Power Posing Before a High-Stakes Social Evaluation.* Harvard Business School.

Chapter 9

1.   Dr Maltz, M. (1960) *Psycho-Cybernetics.*
2.   Napoleon Bonaparte, French military leader.
3.   Kounios, J. (2015) *The Eureka Factor: Aha Moments, Creative Insight and the Brain.* Drexel University.

Chapter 10

1.   Janos Hugo Bruno 'Hans' Selye, pioneering endocrinologist and founder of International Institute of Stress.
2.   Newth, D. *Insights for Managers.*
3.   Prof. Stephen Palmer (Director of the Centre for Stress Management), Co-author with Cary Cooper of *How to Deal with Stress* (2007).
4.   Borstein, S. (1996) *Don't Just Do Something, Sit There.*
5.   Sarah Warber, University of Michigan

Chapter 11

1.   Inaugural address by the President of USA, 1933–45.
2.   General, US Civil War (1861–63).
3.   Albert Ellis, Founder of REBT.
4.   Shindler, J. A (2003) *How to Live 365 Days a Year.*
5.   President of the USA 1861–65.
6.   Goleman, D. (2015) *HBR's 10 Must Reads on Emotional Intelligence.*

List of Exercises

Index